Ss. Cather[ine]
Relig[ion]

God
Yahweh
Allah

What Kids Want to Know:
100 Questions about Faith and Belief

Cover design: Bayard Éditions
Layout: Bayard Éditions and Jessica AuCoin

Published in the United States by
Paulist Press
997 Macarthur Boulevard
Mahwah, NJ 07430

www.paulistpress.com

Originally published in French as *Dieu, Yahweh, Allâh : Les grandes questions sur les trois religions* © 2004, Bayard Éditions Jeunesse, Paris, France

Library of Congress Control Number: 2013954578

ISBN: 978-0-8091-6771-5 (hardcover)

Manufactured in Shenzhen, China in December 2013, by C&C Joint Printing Co., (Guangdong) Ltd.
Job #HN7090

5 4 3 2 1   18   17   16   15   14

Katia Mrowiec • Michel Kubler • Antoine Sfeir

God
Yahweh
Allah

**What Kids Want to Know:
100 Questions about Faith and Belief**

**Illustrations
Olivier André • Gaëtan Évrard • Stéphane Girel • Philippe Poirier**

Paulist Press
New York / Mahwah, NJ

God, Yahweh, Allah

God – what an interesting name! For the millions of men, women and children around the world who say "God" every day, it is a familiar and comforting word. And yet, the one it refers to is quite mysterious. Who is God? How does God reveal himself to us? Do we have to believe in God? And how do we do this? For some believers, God is simply called God; for others, God is called Yahweh or Allah.

Three of the great religions of the world believe in one God: Judaism, Christianity and Islam. Over the centuries, they have developed as majestic branches of the same tree. Each has its own rules, rituals, prayers and feasts.

This book looks at more than 100 questions that young people have asked about these three great religions. Some of their questions are straightforward and have to do with everyday life, such as the foods people are not allowed to eat or the clothes they are expected to wear when they pray. Some questions are about the meaning of major events in people's lives, such as birth, marriage and death, or the mystery of the afterlife. Other questions are about the sometimes terrible images we see in the news, with people using violence in the name of God, turning the profound message of their own religion into something that hurts others.

hree journalists – Katia Mrowiec, Michel Kubler and Antoine Sfeir – have given us answers to these questions. All three of them are passionate about religion in the world today. Using everyday language, they try to explain who God is for Jews, Christians and Muslims, and how believers try to live their faith at each moment of their lives. The authors tell us what they know, using ordinary words, without avoiding delicate subjects, such as the role of women or religious fanaticism.

his book is divided into seven sections: the big questions about God; faith; daily life; prayers and religious practices; feasts and symbols; sacred places; and current issues. In getting to know more about other religions and finding out how other believers live, you will become able to appreciate those who are different from you and how they live in the world.

s you read, you will learn that the greatest value God has taught all believers is respect – for yourself and for others.

NOTE

This book uses the spelling *Muhammad* rather than *Mohammed* when referring to the Prophet, since it is closer to the Arabic pronunciation of his name.

For Hebrew words, the spelling that is closest to the English pronunciation of the word is used: for example, kosher or Sabbath.

Contents

3. Daily life

Chapter 1

The big questions about God

For Jews, Christians and Muslims, there is only one God. But when each of them says God, they don't always mean the same thing!

Who invented God?

As far back in time as we can go, human beings have thought there were powers at work in the world. These powers were seen especially in natural phenomena, such as thunderstorms, earthquakes and floods, and throughout human history in times of famine or war.

To find out more about these powers, which terrified and attracted them at the same time, people tried to understand them. One thing seemed certain: these powers must belong to another world, a world that was very different from the people's everyday lives.

Since people could not control the powers, they tried to figure out who had created them. That is how the name "God" came to be.

But human beings did not invent God the way an inventor creates something new. Most religions will tell you that God came first. God is the creator of the universe.

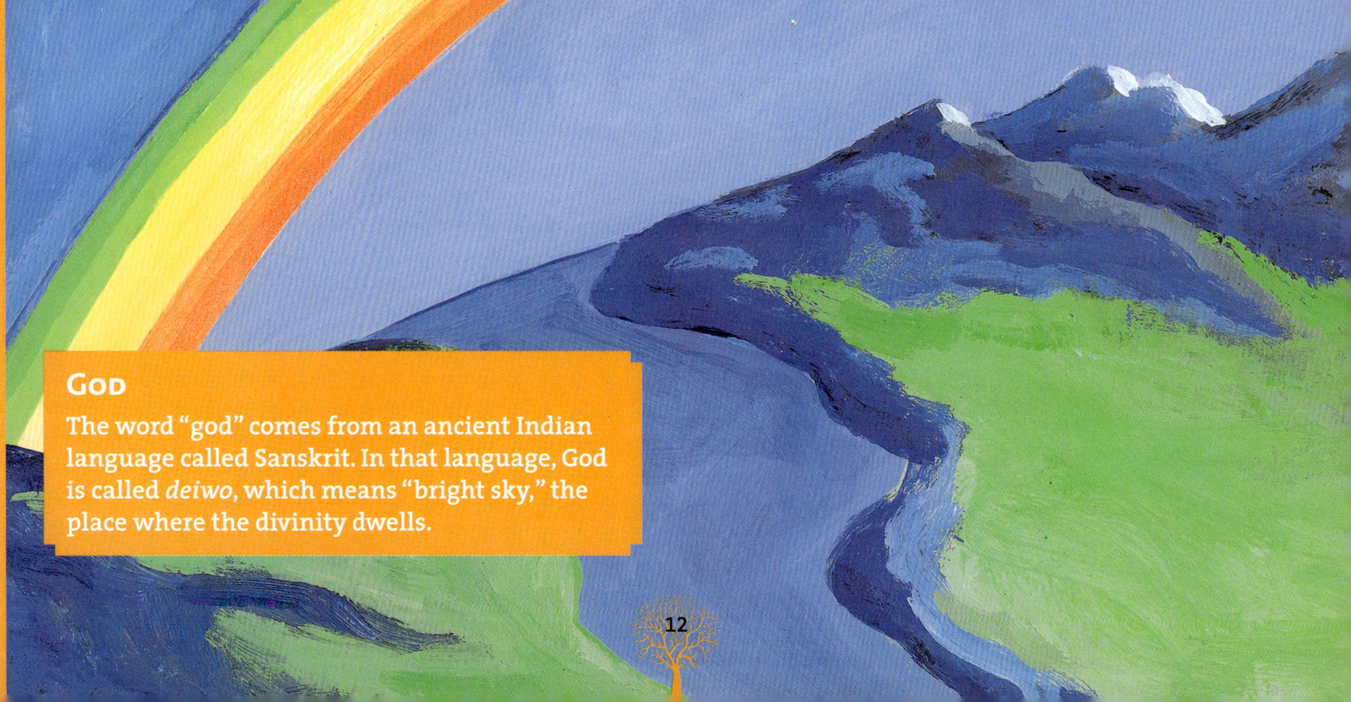

God

The word "god" comes from an ancient Indian language called Sanskrit. In that language, God is called *deiwo*, which means "bright sky," the place where the divinity dwells.

God is eternal, which means God lives outside of time. God has always existed and will exist forever. God is the master of life!

To help them worship and show respect for God, human beings were given certain rules, known as laws or commandments. These rules became part of their daily lives. This is how religions came into being. There are many religions because different peoples have understood God in their own way.

ONE GOD OR MANY GODS?

When the word "god" is used in the plural, we use a small "g". When people believe in more than one god, their religion is called polytheistic, which means "many gods." The Greek and Roman religions of Antiquity were polytheistic. In our day, the traditional religions of Africa and Hinduism are polytheistic.

When people believe in one God (the name begins with a capital "G" because there is only one God), their religion is called monotheistic, which means "one God." Judaism, Christianity and Islam are monotheistic religions.

Who is God ...
for Jews?

For Jews, no word can define God. God is indefinable, the totally Other! And when they try to say what God is like – good, wise, just or almighty, for example – only a part of God's identity is revealed. Yet the Book of Deuteronomy says this: Hear, O Israel: The Lord is our God, the Lord alone (6:4). This sentence contains the entire faith of the Jewish believer (see page 99).

In this way, Jews recognize that God is One, that God is unique, that nothing can divide God. God is eternal, having no beginning and no end. This means that God has always existed and was not created. So God has no age!

But he is also "our God," the God who made a covenant with the people of Israel. God speaks to people, because he asked them to listen. For a Jew, the Word of God is like a precious thread that connects heaven and earth.

When they pray, Jews address God as "our father and our king." They see God as a father who created humankind in his image. This father, the source of all life, showers his children with all his love and kindness. They proclaim God as king, as master and Lord of the universe. In this universe he created, many things attest to God's beauty and majesty: the scent of a rose, the wonder of a rainbow, the grace of a butterfly, the lightness of a breeze, the sweetness of a strawberry.

Who is God ... for Christians?

For Christians, God is the one who created the world and every living thing. God even created human beings in his image. That's what the Book of Genesis, found at the beginning of the Bible, tells us. God appeared to humanity in a very special way. He revealed himself to a tiny group of people – the people of Israel – and made a covenant with them. In this covenant, God promised never to leave them.

But God went even further: God decided to share his life with all human beings by becoming one of them. God sent his son, Jesus, whose name means "God saves."

And so, the God of Christians is the Creator God, the God of the Covenant, and the God who saves – all at the same time.

Christians believe that Jesus is the Son of God who became human. This is called the Incarnation. Jesus called God "Father," and even Abba, which means "Daddy" in his Aramaic language.

In the eyes of Christians, God has the face of a Father because he is the master of the world, the face of a Son because in Jesus of Nazareth he became human, and also the face of a Spirit. The Spirit is the breath of life who gave birth to the whole universe and who, still today, is given to all who ask for him. God is Father, Son and Holy Spirit. This is called the Trinity (see page 55).

People could say many things about God: God is infinite and all-powerful, good and merciful. But the best definition is that God is love. God loves every person and asks all people to share in this love.

Who is God ... for Muslims?

Muslim is an Arabic word that means "one who surrenders to God."

In Arabic, God is called Allah, which means "God alone." God is one, eternal, without equal. Because Allah is also the First and the Last, nothing can be compared to Allah.

The Qur'an says, "He is God, the One, God, the Self-sufficient One. He does not give birth, nor was He born, and there is nothing like Him" (*sura* 112, verses 1–4). Allah has 99 names; the hundredth name is the one that no one may say.

Are God, Yahweh and Allah the same God?

Jews, Christians and Muslims do not address God in the same way. Jews do not say God's name out loud (see page 44), and Muslims say "Allah." But is it still the same God? Yes … and no! Most importantly, the answer is yes, since here it has to do with God's name in the three religions: if a Jew, a Christian or a Muslim claims that his God is not the same as the God of the other two, that would imply either that for him there are other gods (which means he is no longer a monotheist) or that the God of the others does not exist (which shows a serious lack of respect for another believer).

But when a Jew, a Christian or a Muslim speaks of "God," they don't necessarily mean the same thing. It's as if each religion looks at God with its own glasses, even though it says that God is one. There is only one God, but one can describe God in dozens of different ways.

For a Jew, God is described as "I am who I am," meaning that they cannot really describe God at all. And for a Muslim, Allah is the one and only God, who cannot be compared to anything.

Beyond the names we give God, God mainly differs from one religious tradition to another by the qualities that people attribute to him, by the role he is expected to play, and even in the way he is spoken to in prayer. Some of these differences are minor, but others are so big that you might sometimes wonder if Jews, Christians and Muslims really do worship the same God!

Why do people say that **Abraham** is the **father** of all **believers**?

It's true. When we compare the three great religions that believe in one God, we often say that what they have in common is Abraham, the father of all believers.

For Muslims, as for the faithful of the other religions, Abraham (in Arabic, *Ibrahim*) is the one responsible for monotheism, or belief in one God. For Jews and Christians, Abraham obeyed God; he surrendered himself to God, even agreeing to sacrifice his son Isaac as God asked. For Muslims it was not Isaac but Ishmael, the first-born son of Ibrahim, whom he had with Hagar, his Egyptian servant.

What's the **difference** between a **Hebrew**, a **Jew** and an **Israelite**?

A Hebrew is a descendant of Abraham. About 4,000 years ago, God told Abraham to leave his home country and go to Canaan, which was also called the Promised Land. To get there he had to cross a large river, the Euphrates. Later on, the descendants of his people became known as Hebrews, which means "the people from beyond" the river.

"Israeli" is a recent word. It describes the people who live in the state of Israel, which was created in 1948.

An Israelite is a member of the people of Israel. Jacob was Abraham's grandson. One day God changed Jacob's name to Israel, which means "God rules." Jacob had twelve sons, and each became the head of a tribe. These twelve tribes of Israel made up the Hebrew people. Later, Moses freed the Hebrews, who had become slaves of Pharaoh, the king of Egypt. This event marked the birth of a new nation, which took its name from the people's common ancestor, Israel. Jacob's story is told in the Book of Genesis.

A Jew is a believer who follows the Law of Moses. In 587 B.C., the Israelites were deported to Babylon. When they returned from this exile 50 years later, they settled in Judea, in the land of Judah, the largest of the twelve tribes of Israel. The name "Jew" was given to the people who lived in Judea and to those who observed the Law of Moses.

"JEW": A NAME THAT DESERVES RESPECT

You may have heard the term "Jew" used as an insult. This racist behaviour is very serious because it shows no respect for the Jewish faith. The Jews have suffered a great deal throughout their history because people have not respected their beliefs.

Where does the name "Christian" come from?

Christian means "disciple of Christ." In Greek, the word *Christos* means "messiah": the one sent by God through whom humanity will be saved. For many people of Jesus' time, whether they were Jews or not, Jesus was that messiah and they believed in him. We often call him "Jesus Christ," but "Christ" is not Jesus' last name (see page 49). It is the title given to him because he was sent by God.

After Jesus' death and resurrection, his disciples gathered in various places: in Jerusalem, of course, but also in Ephesus (now in Turkey), in Corinth (in Greece), in Rome, and elsewhere. The Acts of the Apostles (chapter 11, verse 26) says that in one of these cities, Antioch (today found in Turkey), the people called the followers of Christ "Christians" for the first time. They were making fun of Jesus' followers. But Christ's followers soon adopted the name and it spread all around the Mediterranean.

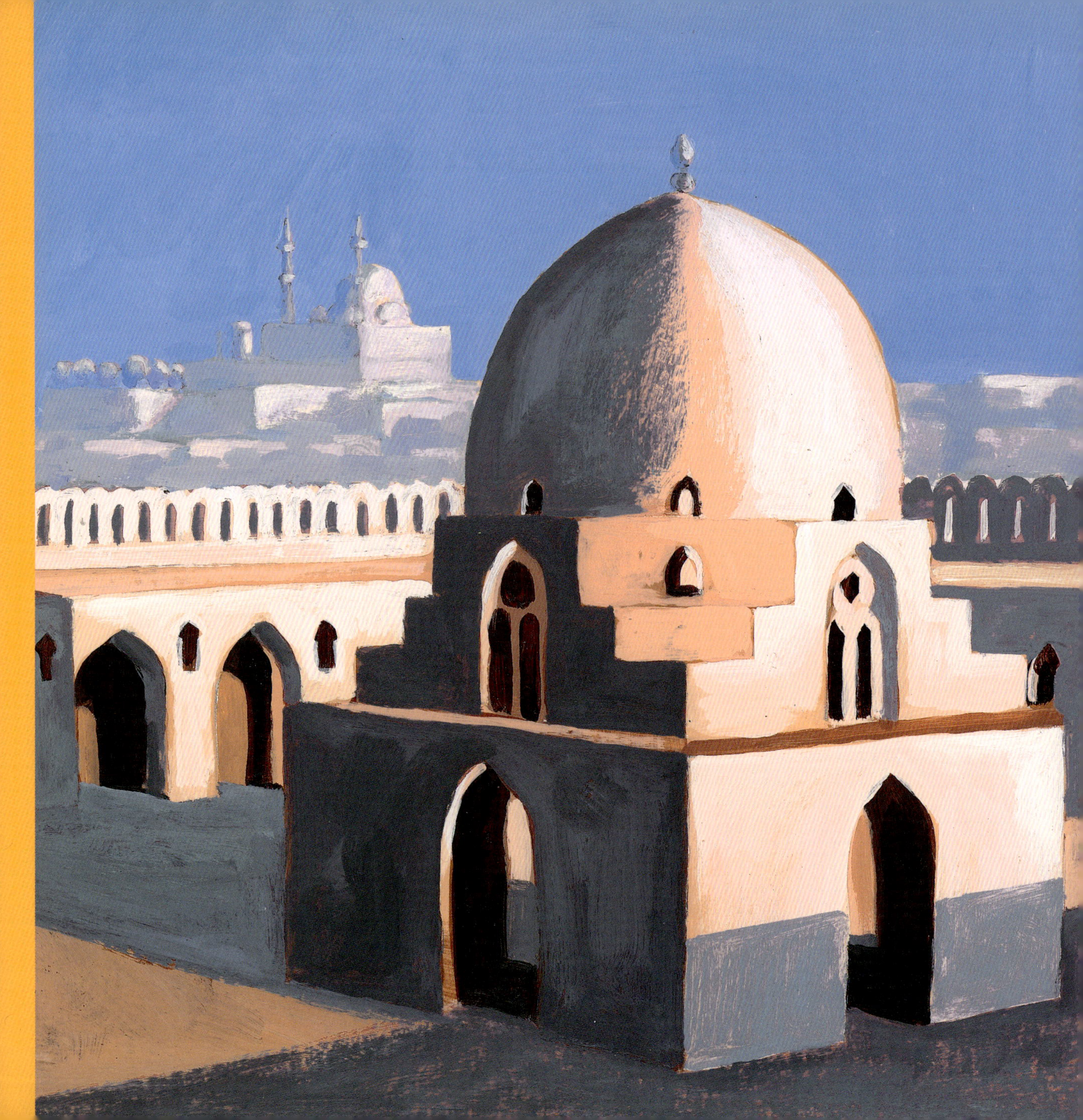

Muslim, Islam: what do these words mean?

Muslim is an Arabic word that means "someone who surrenders themselves to God."

The word "Islam" comes from the Arabic root *slm*, meaning "peace" or "health." It refers to the religion of those who surrender themselves to God.

The prophet Muhammad, the founder of Islam, told Christians and Jews, "I came to perfect your religion." He then explained that Jews and Christians had received messages from God but had turned away from them. According to Muhammad, he asked God that Islam become the religion of everyone. Before his death Muhammad said, "I am the seal of the prophets." He meant that he was the last of the prophets; there would be no more after him.

What's the difference between a Muslim and an Islamist?

To better understand the difference between these terms, we need to go back to Muhammad, the founder of Islam. On several occasions he heard a voice that kept saying, "Read" (in Arabic, *ikra'*). It was the archangel Gabriel telling him to read the Word of God and tell others about it. In Arabic, this recitation is known as "Qur'an." It remained oral well after the death of the Prophet in 632. But 20 years later, the third successor to Muhammad (in Arabic, a successor is called a *khalife*, which gave us the word "caliph" to describe Muhammad's successors) reunited Muhammad's last companions. He had them write out the Word of God, which God had transmitted to his messenger Muhammad through the archangel Gabriel. So that believers could learn the Qur'an by heart, it was written in order from the longest to the shortest sura, or chapter.

By doing it this way, the scribes who wrote out the Qur'an mixed up the years of Muhammad's preaching. But, once it was written, it could no longer be changed. The scribes had clearly made the Qur'an so difficult to read that it became necessary to interpret some of the more complicated passages. In Arabic, this attempt at interpretation was called *ijtihad*. Several schools of interpretation came into being. In the eighth century, great scholars founded famous schools that gave birth to several religious movements that still exist today. But in the ninth century, the doors were closed on *ijtihad*, and even today, Muslims are not allowed to interpret the Qur'an.

The book of the Qur'an is divided into many chapters, called suras.

There is a world of difference between a Muslim and an Islamist. In the nineteenth century, a great French writer called Chateaubriand was already talking about Islamism. But, for him, that simply meant "Islam."

Today, when we speak of Islamism, we are talking about Muslims who are trying to make an entire society Islamic. This religious movement may

attack the administration of a country and public authorities as well as the foundation of society, such as the family or the school system. It has slowly grown throughout the world since the 1980s.

Islamism settles for a simplified reading of the Qur'an. This movement was influenced by a school of thought known as the Hanbalite school. Its point of view can be summed up in one sentence: "After the Prophet, there is nothing new."

What is a **prophet**?

A prophet is someone who spreads the Word of God to humankind. The message can be good news, or it can be a warning or a criticism about how people are living.

It is God who calls the prophet, usually in a dream or a vision. God gives the prophet the mission of carrying God's Word to men and women, and often to kings, so they will change their behaviour. God said to the prophet Jeremiah: "I have put my words in your mouth" (Jeremiah 1:9). As God's spokesperson, the prophet also has the mission of helping and defending the poor and all who suffer because of injustice.

There are Jewish, Christian and Muslim prophets.

What is a prophet ... for a Jew?

The prophets are very important people in the history of Israel. When the people were not living as God asked, the prophet reminded them of the wonders God had done for them: God freed them from slavery and gave them a new land. But when the people suffered greatly because of war, deportation or famine, the prophet encouraged them to stay faithful to God. In the Bible, Moses, Samuel, Isaiah, Jeremiah and Ezekiel are some of the greatest prophets.

... for a Christian?

Like the Jews, Christians recognized the importance of the Word of God that the prophets spoke to them. In the Gospels, a new person stepped forward – John the Baptist. He was the last of the prophets, the one who announced the coming of the Son of God. John recognized this Messiah in the person of Jesus. From then on, God no longer needed prophets: his son Jesus is the living Word, the Word that "became flesh," as John the evangelist put it (John 1:14).

... for a **Muslim**?

Moses and Jesus are two of the 25 prophets mentioned in the Qur'an. For Muslims, these men of God received messages that were authentic but incomplete or not always understood. Muhammad is considered to be the greatest prophet because God entrusted his entire message to him.

Why are there different kinds of Christians: Catholics, Protestants, Orthodox and Anglicans?

At first, all Christians formed one family. This is what Jesus wanted, since he asked his disciples to announce his message, or Gospel (in Greek, this means "good news"), to all nations so that all people would believe in him.

Among the first Christians, some were Jews, and others were pagans who did not believe in the God of Israel. Together, in the rural areas and in the cities, they formed groups called churches. Each group was led by an "elder" (in Greek, *presbyteros*, which gave us the word "priest"). But these small churches soon combined with the five large cities of the Roman Empire that became the five capitals of Christianity. The most important of these cities was Rome, which always enjoyed special privileges because the apostles Peter and Paul died there. The other cities were Constantinople (today Istanbul, in Turkey), Jerusalem, Antioch (in Turkey) and Alexandria (in Egypt).

Tensions arose among the five churches when they tried to answer questions such as these: How can Jesus Christ be human and divine at the same time? How should Christians live? When their answers were different, the churches began to argue with each other. Political rivalries made things even more complicated. Some groups decided to leave. That is how different Christian churches came into being.

From the fifth century on, the Eastern churches (especially around Antioch and Alexandria) cut

themselves off from the others. Later, in the eleventh century, there was a schism (a strong and lasting separation) between Eastern and Western Christians, because the Eastern Churches no longer accepted the authority of Rome. There were now two main branches of Christianity: Catholicism (a word that means "universal Church") in the West, and Orthodoxy ("right belief") in the East.

In the sixteenth century, a movement formed against the authority of the pope. It called for spiritual "reform" and a return to the Gospel. Started by the German priest Martin Luther and the French reformer John Calvin, this movement became known as Protestantism. It developed into several families (Lutherans, Baptists, and others). Anglicanism arose at the same time, after a break in relations between the king of England and the pope.

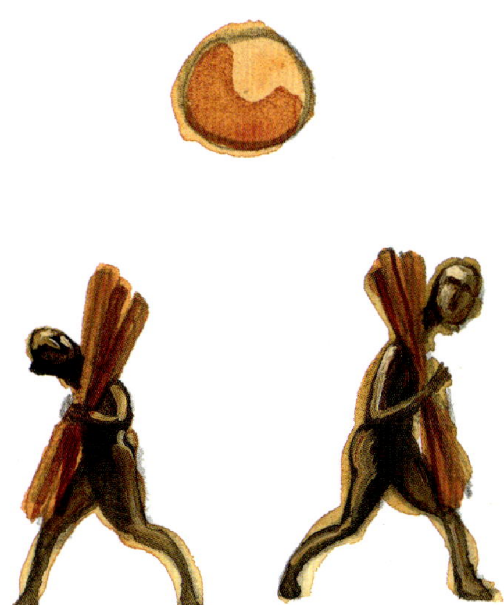

Chapter 2

Faith

God spoke to people and revealed his identity to some of them.
Jewish, Christian and Muslim faithful have tried to understand
what God wanted to say to them.

Who invented the Jewish religion?

Is religion invented in a laboratory? No – it's an experiment, but it takes place in the human heart.

For the Jews, the Bible is the Word of God. It tells the history of those who set out in search of God. Three important people shaped Judaism.

The first is Abraham. He was a nomad who lived among many peoples that believed in several gods. But Abraham thought that God was One. This is called a revelation. Abraham entered into a surprising friendship with his God. Most importantly, he discovered that God was part of human life, promising to be faithful to the people. The Bible calls this the Covenant.

A few centuries later, on Mount Sinai, God gave Moses the Ten Commandments and the Torah, which is the Law. The Law is the foundation for the Jewish people. It contains laws about worship and other things that help Jews to lead lives that keep them close to God.

Much later, in the fifth century B.C., the priest Ezra reorganized religious life. Worship now took place in the synagogue and followed certain rules, the readings from the Torah were now done three times a week, and Jews were no longer allowed to marry non-Jews. For historians, this is when Judaism as we know it today was born.

Who **wrote** the Bible?

The Bible was written by the Jewish people. They may not have built pyramids or cathedrals, but the Jewish people have given humanity an amazing masterpiece that is as valuable as any great monument.

The Bible is not a single book written from start to finish by one and the same person. It's really a small library that brings together many works by different authors. We can identify some of the authors, but many remain anonymous.

Among these authors are scribes who wrote the royal histories and the laws. Other authors include priests, who composed sermons, teachings and prayers, as well as poets and philosophers. It is even possible that certain kings wrote books of prayers and hymns. Finally, there are the prophets whose followers wrote down their words.

Book after book, page after page (you could even say scroll after scroll, because the texts were originally written on long parchment scrolls), each of the authors made their small contribution to the whole Bible.

The whole Bible wasn't put together all at once. For one thing, the writers didn't live in the same place or at the same time. They did their work at the request of kings or priests. They gathered together the oral traditions – what was handed down by word of mouth – and collected ancient writings to make sure they would not be forgotten. This work of compiling took nearly ten centuries! The goal of the scribes was not to prepare a report on what happened in the world since Creation, but to show that God was present in human life in many ways.

DID GOD WRITE THE BIBLE?

For Jews and Christians, the Bible is the Word of God. This means that biblical writings carry the stamp of the Creator God. Of course, human hands composed the texts in a particular language, first Hebrew and then Greek. But these texts are not the fruit of the writers' imagination. The Spirit of God guided their hearts and minds so they could better express what God wanted to say to humanity. That is why believers say the Bible is an inspired book.

Who is Jesus for Jews?

According to Flavius Josephus, a first-century Jewish historian, "Jesus was a wise man of good conduct." But, in general, the Jews see Jesus as a Jew like any other Jew, and nothing more.

For them, Jesus cannot be the Son of God because they believe in the absolute unity of God. God is one and indivisible. One God in three persons, Father, Son and Spirit, is unthinkable for the Jews. They also believe that God does not have a body. To say that God could become human was a real scandal for the Jews.

Nor was Jesus the Messiah that the Jews were expecting. The one they were waiting for would bring to the Earth the glory of God, universal peace and a kingdom of justice. Men and women would live as brothers and sisters, and all would acknowledge God. For the Jews, the coming of Jesus brought neither peace nor happiness to the Earth. The Jews do not see Jesus as a prophet, either. What he said could not be God's Word because he strayed too far from the Law of Moses. Even though Jesus said, "I have not come to abolish the Law but to fulfill it," his words were seen as reformist, because they changed the way people understood the Law. Remember, for the Jews, the Word of God is eternal; it never grows old or needs updating.

For Jews, what is there after death?

Jews believe in eternal life with God, because God, who is the source of all life, cannot allow death to have the last word. For Jews, the human being is both a body and a soul. Both belong to the Creator. After death, the body returns to the ground. The soul rejoins God, the source from which the soul had detached to give life to the body. There, the soul enjoys eternal happiness, as the images of "garden" and "feast" suggest. This happiness depends on the merits of each person and is available to all who are "righteous," even those who belong to other religions. Those who keep doing wicked and unjust things will be condemned to oblivion.

For Jews, life on earth is priceless because this is where each person can and must show that they are trying to become "righteous and holy." A famous rabbi used to compare life to an entrance hall where people put on their best clothes, meaning the good that they do, before entering into the banquet hall of heaven.

The resurrection of the dead is also at the centre of the Jewish faith. It will happen when the Messiah, the One sent by God, arrives. Then the "world to come," where the divine Presence will light up the whole Earth, will appear. Each person will then be able to gaze upon the Creator face to face.

Why do Jews **study** the Bible?

Jews study the Bible to imprint the words of God in their hearts.

Faithful Jews are always hungry for the Word of God. For them, the Bible is sweet like milk and honey, and its words are a true delight. In the Book of Deuteronomy, it is even written that "one does not live by bread alone, but by every word that comes from the mouth of the Lord" (8:3).

Studying the Bible, and especially the Torah, is the first commandment. Even today, faithful Jews set aside a few minutes every day to study the texts, analyze them and probe them until they know them by heart.

Torah is a Hebrew word that means "law," or, to be more precise, "instruction" or "teaching."

Parents pass on to their children this appetite for the Torah. Studying is first done in the home, and then at the synagogue, or sometimes at special schools called *yeshivas*.

WHAT IS THE TORAH?

The Torah is the first five books of the Bible. It tells the stories of the creation of the world, the life of Abraham, Isaac and Jacob, the adventures of the Hebrews in Egypt, their flight from that country, their wandering in the desert, the gift of the Ten Commandments, and their arrival in the Promised Land.

The written Torah, called the "Law of Moses," contains the essential rules of Judaism. The oral Torah was all the spoken words that sought to put into practice the Law of Moses. At first these teachings were passed on orally from master to disciple. Later they were written down to form the *Talmud*, which means "study" in Hebrew.

What **commandment** must Jews **respect**?

The commandment that Jews must respect is the Torah that God gave Moses on Mount Sinai. The Ten Commandments are found there, along with 613 other commandments of the Jewish tradition. Called *mitzvoth*, they form a code of conduct toward God, oneself, other human beings, and even animals and nature. By respecting these commandments, the faithful become aware that everything belongs to God and everything comes from God. The commandments are signposts that make the world more beautiful and more holy and add a little eternal life into daily life.

Among the 613 commandments, there are 365 prohibitions and 248 obligations. The number 365 equals the number of days it takes for the Earth to revolve around the sun: these are small steps on the right path that leads to God. The number 248 equals the parts of the human body; all are essential for life, just like the Torah.

Here are a few examples of obligations: love your neighbour, start a family, respect life, be honest in business, observe the Sabbath, eat kosher foods, do not defile the Lord's name.

In a life-or-death situation, the Torah is set aside. Believers are expected to break the commandments to save their own life or another person's life.

Why don't Jews say God's name?

In the Bible, to name someone is to have power over that person. When Adam named each of the living beings that God put before him, Adam gained power over them. To change someone's name is also to take "ownership" of that person. God acted this way with Abram. When God sent him on mission, God changed Abram's name to Abraham. And to know the name of one's enemy in the Bible is to have already captured him.

To look at it the other way, when you tell someone your name, you reveal a little part of yourself. You do this to show that you trust and like this person. God dared to do that. In the well-known story of the burning bush, God revealed his own name to Moses, as to a friend. God said, "I am who I am," and then added, "You shall say to the Israelites 'I am' has sent me to you" (Exodus 3:14).

"I am" is a strange name, isn't it? God is someone who cannot be confined by a name. The name God calls himself is so mysterious, it causes lots of problems for translators! By using that name, God is saying this about himself: "Yes, I exist, but I won't stand idly by, just watching you live. I am and I remain with you."

Out of respect for God, Jews do not take God's name in vain or say it for no reason.

Do Jews have the same Bible as Christians?

We should ask instead if Christians have the same Bible as Jews! At the beginning, the Bible was a collection of Jewish texts. Most of them are common to both Jews and Christians.

Imagine for a minute that the Bible is a real library. On the top shelf are the five books of the Torah.

On the second shelf are the books of the prophets, which are easy to recognize because the prophet's name is often in the title. These books also tell the story of the Kingdom of Israel and contain a few very colourful stories, such as Sampson's adventures or David's battle with Goliath.

The third shelf includes all sorts of writings: prayers and hymns of praise like the Psalms, books of wisdom, historical accounts, and even a love poem, the Canticle of Canticles.

To this collection Christians added a new shelf of seven books, written in Greek, which brings the Old Testament to an end.

In their Bible, Christians have another "library" called the New Testament. Here you can find the four Gospels, which tell the story of Jesus' life, as well as many letters of instruction and other writings.

What do Christians **believe**?

In God, of course! God first revealed himself to the Jewish people, but, for Christians, God also had a human face: Jesus of Nazareth, the Son of God.

The God of Christians is the one God – the God of Abraham, Isaac and Jacob, to whom God revealed himself, and the God of Jesus, in whom he became a human being or, to put it another way, in whom he was incarnated.

To express their faith in God, Christians recite the Creed, from the Latin word *credo*, which means "I believe." The Creed, which is a summary of what Christians believe, was written in the fourth century.

To be a Christian is to believe in "God, the Father almighty, Creator of heaven and earth." God was at the origin of all that lives: the entire universe (the Earth, the planets, the stars) that was formed millions of years ago, as well as every living being ever born. God is Father because he is the one who gives life and because, for each of his creatures, he has the never-ending love of a father for his children. In God's eyes, every human being has value. When Christians say that God is "almighty," it

is not because God possesses some supernatural power, but because God overflows with love for everyone.

To be a Christian is to believe "in Jesus Christ, his only Son, our Lord, who was conceived by the Holy Spirit, born of the Virgin Mary, was crucified, died ... and on the third day he rose again from the dead." God loves human beings so much that he wanted to save them from anything that stops them from living in peace: evil, sins that lead human beings away from God, and death. To do this, God decided to become one of us. He sent his son Jesus, born of his Spirit in the womb of a young woman named Mary. God didn't just pretend to be human. He lived his life to the very end, accepting to be condemned by human beings to the point of dying on a cross. This is known as the crucifixion. To show all people that they could be saved, God raised Jesus from the dead. This is called the resurrection.

To be a Christian is to believe in "the Holy Spirit ... the giver of life." The Holy Spirit is the power of God that has been present since the world began and that

underlies the origin of the Church, the community of Christians.

Once they have expressed their faith in God who is Father, Son and Holy Spirit, Christians add that they believe in a Church that is "one, holy, catholic [which means universal, for everyone] and apostolic [which means founded on the apostles, the first friends of Jesus]." They also believe in the forgiveness of sins: God can free human beings from the evil they have done. Finally, they believe in the resurrection of the dead for eternity: their life will have no end.

But the faith of Christians is not only about agreeing to a set of doctrines; it is above all about the believer's personal relationship with God. For Christians, God is not an abstract idea, but someone who is alive, someone they can talk to, someone who listens to everything they say.

Why is there a New Testament in the Christian Bible?

In the Bible, the word "testament" comes from a Greek word that means "covenant." What Christians call the "Old Testament" is a collection of books that forms the first part of the Bible. These books tell of the "first covenant" that God made with the people of Israel. (For Jews, this collection forms most of the Bible.)

The first part of the Christian Bible is called "old" because it deserves great reverence, but also because God came to conclude a "new" covenant, and therefore a "new testament," by sending his Son, Jesus the Christ, to live among human beings. From that point on, God made a covenant not only with the Jewish people but with all the peoples of the Earth.

The New Testament contains different documents that tell why and how Jesus is truly the Messiah, the one sent by God, whose coming was announced by the Old Testament. There are four Gospels (this Greek word means "good news"), the Acts of the Apostles (which describes the birth of the Church after Jesus is gone), and letters, especially from Saint Paul, addressed to the Christian communities that had just started in Asia Minor (now Turkey), Greece and Rome. The New Testament does not replace the Old. Just the opposite! It completes the Old Testament and gives it new meaning. Christians believe that certain people and events in the Bible of the Jews directly announce the coming of Christ.

Is "Christ" Jesus' last name?

No. Even though people are used to saying "Jesus Christ" in the same breath, it is not two first names that go together, like John Paul or Anne Marie, or even a first name and a last name.

As was the custom in those days, people called him "Jesus of Nazareth" to connect him with the town where his family lived.

The word "Christ" comes from the Greek verb meaning "to anoint." This is the same word that, in Hebrew, refers to the Messiah, the one the people of Israel are waiting for, the one who will come from God at the end of time to put an end to sickness, suffering and war. In the Gospels, the apostle Peter is the first to affirm that Jesus of Nazareth is this Messiah. Peter is the first to call him Jesus the Christ.

From the word "Christ" comes the term "Christian," which refers to those who, like Saint Peter, believe that Jesus is the Messiah.

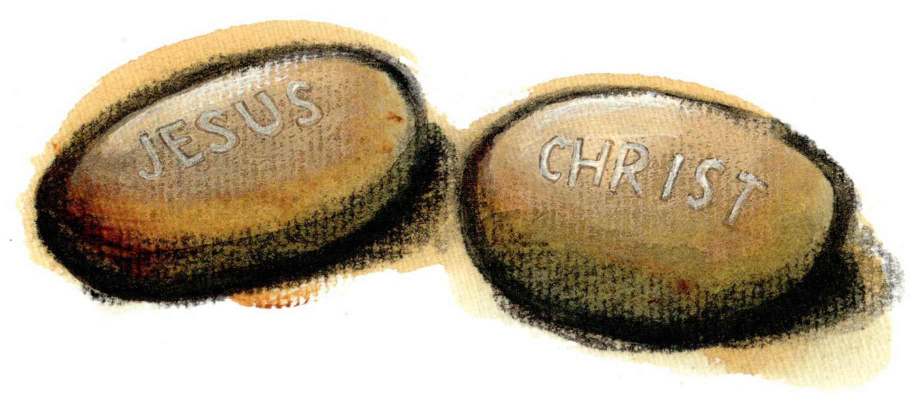

Why do Christians say that **Christ** is **risen**?

The Gospels tell us that, after his death on a cross, on the Friday after the Jewish Passover, the body of Jesus was placed in a tomb. But, on the morning of the third day after his death, the women who came to anoint his body found the tomb open and empty. They heard an angel tell them that Jesus had "risen."

This word comes from Latin and means "awakened" or "raised up." It means that a person who was dead is alive again. Jesus appeared alive to a number of his disciples and friends; he spoke to them, ate with them, and even performed some miracles.

Before his death, to prove to people that he was divine, Jesus had "raised" several people, like his friend Lazarus and the widow's son. But their bodies remained mortal, and these people later died again.

On Easter morning, Jesus showed that he was truly alive. Christians believe it is God who raised him to show that death was now defeated, thanks to the sacrifice of his Son. Jesus went to the very limits of his love for humankind by giving himself up to the torture of the cross: he showed that love is stronger than death. Christians believe that all people can achieve this same victory: all are called to rise again to new life in God.

"

Did Jesus invent a religion?

The Christian religion rests on this basic belief: "Christ died for our sins. He was buried and raised on the third day. He appeared to Peter and then to the Twelve." This is what Saint Paul wrote in his first letter to the Christians in the city of Corinth (chapter 15). Paul didn't say that Jesus invented a religion or even that he decided to start a religious group that was different from all those that existed already. But Christians did define themselves as the community of all those who agreed with the statement that Saint Paul made about Jesus. This community was not born overnight, as some associations or political parties are.

Jesus was Jewish, and he never gave up the faith of his ancestors. But his idea of religion was quite different from that of the religious leaders of his time, who jealously clung to their power and made deals with the Roman occupiers. Also, Jesus was aware of being the one God sent to fulfill the promises made by his Father to the people of Israel. He was hurt by those among the Jews who refused to recognize him as the Messiah. This refusal was without doubt the main cause of his arrest and death.

At first, all of Christ's disciples – the first "Christians" – were Jewish. They continued to observe the commandments of Judaism and to go to the synagogue to pray, but they would also get together privately to remember Jesus, their Lord. Before long, pagans (non-Jews) accepted Jesus' message and became Christians, too. In the emerging Church, there was a mix: some were Jews and some were pagans. An important question arose: did the Christians who had been pagan first have to become Jews like Jesus before becoming Christians? Influenced by Saint Peter, and especially Saint Paul, it was decided that they didn't. At this moment, Christianity as a religion was born. New Christians came more and more from the pagan world, and Christianity separated from Judaism.

What is the **message** of Jesus?

As soon as he began to speak in public, around the age of 30, he impressed people with his great natural authority and the power of his words. He spoke in God's name and proclaimed a message of joy for the poor, healing for the sick, and freedom for prisoners. But he didn't just make nice speeches. His actions supported his words: he healed many who were sick and performed extraordinary signs, like the multiplication of the loaves and the miraculous catch of fish. He wanted to awaken the faith of those who asked for it.

In acting this way, Jesus was announcing the coming of the Kingdom of God. This was the heart of his message. The Kingdom of God had nothing to do with the idea of a king in his palace who rules over a land. This Kingdom of God even went against some of the religious ideas of Jesus' time. In God's kingdom, God shows his preference for the poor and the weak, and he expects everyone not only to love their neighbour as themselves, as was written in the Old Testament, but also to love their enemies! Jesus left a brand new commandment: "Love one another as I have loved you." To be a Christian is to be ready, like Jesus, to give one's life for others.

Jesus asked those who wanted to follow him always to remember what he endured and suffered for them, especially by repeating the actions of his sacrifice for the world. This is called the sacrament of the eucharist, and means that Jesus is always living in their midst. He also asked them not to keep for themselves all that they had received from him, but to go out into the whole world to proclaim his good news, the Gospel. This message must be made known throughout the entire world because it concerns all people, who are saved from sin and death by the Christ.

Why do Christians say that Mary is the Mother of God?

First of all, it isn't to turn the Virgin Mary into some kind of goddess! The Christian faith proclaims that it was by the Holy Spirit, and not a man, that Mary conceived Jesus. The angel had announced the news by saying that the child was the Son of God – that God himself would become human to rule over humankind. Mary agreed to be the mother of this child, even though she did not see herself as the mother of God. She raised Jesus as every mother raises her child, with affection and discipline, asking herself lots of questions about what he would become when he grew up.

Mary was a simple young woman of faith who obeyed an extraordinary call from God. When Christians say she is the Mother of God, it is not to award her with some kind of medal, but to say that her son was, from his conception, God himself in human flesh. This statement was drafted in a time (the fifth century) when some Christians wrongly thought that Jesus was not God, but that he became God later for having given his life out of love for humankind.

To say that Mary is the mother of God is a way of emphasizing that Jesus, from his conception and birth, was at the same time truly divine and truly human. This belief is at the heart of the Christian faith.

Who is the **Holy** Spirit?

In the opening pages of the Bible, in the Book of Genesis, "the Spirit of God" is there, hovering over the waters at the moment of the world's creation. Each time God begins something very important, it is his Spirit at work. And when God gives someone like a king, a prophet or even the Virgin Mary an important mission, he sends his Holy Spirit. The Holy Spirit is the breath of God, his life force.

The Spirit is present in the life of Jesus. When Jesus is baptized in the Jordan River, he sees the skies open and the Holy Spirit descend on him in the form of a dove. Later on he will apply to himself these words of the prophet Isaiah: "The Spirit of God is upon me, he has sent me to bring the Good News to the poor" (Isaiah 61:1). Later on, as he is leaving his disciples, Jesus promises to send the Holy Spirit to inspire them to say and do things in his name after he is gone. This is what happened on the day of Pentecost: the apostles, hiding in a house in Jerusalem, receive the gift of the Spirit, which comes upon them as tongues of fire. Filled with courage, they go out to announce that Jesus is alive. Those who have come from all parts of the world hear and understand the apostles – each in their own language!

For Christians, the Holy Spirit, who is known as the "third person" of the Trinity (with the Father and the Son), acts as a fire that purifies the heart and sets it ablaze. The Spirit is always active in the world, even in places where Jesus is unknown.

Is the **Trinity** three gods?

No! If the Trinity were three gods, that would mean that Christians no longer believe in one God.

The Trinity is one of the most difficult parts of the Christian faith to understand. For Christians, the Trinity is at the heart of their faith, but Jews and Muslims strongly oppose this belief. In God, who is one, there are three truly distinct persons, but they are all of the same divine nature. There is the Father, the Son (the Word of God), and the Holy Spirit, who expresses the relationship of love between the Father and the Son. This means that God himself is already a set of relationships. God is singular, but can only be defined in the plural!

This is why God placed human beings at the highest point of creation. God probably didn't want to be all alone. And, since God is love, he created the world, the man and the woman to love them. For Christians, believing in the Trinity is believing in a God who is filled with love. And it is "in the name of the Father and of the Son and of the Holy Spirit" (Matthew 28:19) that Christians are called to baptize all nations.

What do Muslims believe?

For a Muslim, "there is no God but Allah." But there is a slight difference. When Muslims say, "There is no God but Allah," they express their belief in one God, just like the other monotheistic religions, but they emphasize the oneness of God. Why? Because Christians believe in the Trinity (see page 55): God the Father, the Son Jesus, and the Holy Spirit. Islam rejects this belief. It accuses Christians of being *mushrikun* – polytheists. The Qur'an says that "He is God ... the Self-sufficient One. He does not give birth, nor was he born" (*sura* 112). No one is equal to God.

But the faith of Muslims identifies duties: the Five Pillars, the commandments that the whole community must observe (see page 60).

Muslims believe in angels, prophets, revealed books, and the Last Judgment. They believe that certain prophets brought revealed books with them: for example, Moses and the Torah, and Jesus and the Gospels. This is why Islam considers Jews and Christians to be "people of the Book." Muslims believe in heaven (see page 63) and also in Satan *(Shaitan)* and hell.

Islam does not have sacraments or clergy: the believer is alone before Allah.

Who *invented* Islam?

Islam was not "invented." It was handed down by a man, Muhammad, who is also called the Prophet (see page 58). His job was to lead caravans across the desert. When he was 40 years old, Muhammad heard the voice of the archangel Gabriel saying to him, "*Iqra,*" which means "recite" or "read" in Arabic. Muhammad began to recite the Word of God that the archangel Gabriel dictated to him. He then passed on the Word of God to his companions orally.

Qur'an, *in Arabic, means "recitation" or "reading"*

Each companion then passed on this recitation of the Word of God to others.

WHY IS MUHAMMAD CALLED THE PROPHET?

Because he received the revelation, the knowledge, of the divine word. He is also above the other prophets because he alone had the privilege of receiving this revelation through the archangel Gabriel, the transmitter of the Word of God.

Did **Muhammad** write the **Qur'an**?

No. The words that the archangel Gabriel dictated to him, Muhammad preached orally until his death in 632. He did this preaching in two periods: from 610 to 622, and then from 622 to 632.

The first period of preaching took place in his hometown, Mecca. This town was in the desert of the Arabian Peninsula on the routes used by caravans, which came from India along the famous Silk Road, transporting spices and fabrics to the region that is today known as the Near East. Some of the caravans went up to Mesopotamia, known as Iraq today.

At that time, the rich tribe that ruled Mecca believed in many gods. Each product transported by the caravans had its own god or goddess to whom the people offered gifts. You can imagine that Muhammad's first sermons would have upset the town's rich business owners, because Muhammad criticized their luxurious lifestyle.

Fortunately, Muhammad could count on the protection of two people: his wife, Khadijah, and his uncle, Abu Talib. Khadijah ran a business: she was the owner of the caravans Muhammad worked for. Abu Talib had welcomed Muhammad into his home at the age of six, when his parents died and he became an orphan. Abu Talib's son, Ali, was the Prophet's cousin. He became one of Muhammad's first companions and married his cherished daughter, Fatima. Ali would carry on the work of the Prophet.

After the death of his two protectors, in 622, Mohammad was driven out of Mecca.

During his first period of preaching, the Prophet mostly spoke of human beings' relationship with God (Allah), the Creator.

After he was banished, Muhammad found refuge in the town of Yathrib, 500 kilometres north of Mecca. He later renamed it Medina. Here he began his second period of preaching. His sermons focused on people's relationship to each other. This is why Muhammad announced a series of social, religious, economic and political rules.

The successors of the Prophet, the caliphs, were both earthly and spiritual rulers of the faithful, and they used this power to promote the expansion of Islam.

The third successor of Muhammad, the caliph Othman, reunited the last of the Prophet's companions in 652 and asked them to write out the Qur'an. To make recitation easier, the Qur'an was written from the longest to the shortest *sura* (a *sura* is a chapter of the Qur'an).

What are the Five Pillars of faith for Muslims?

The Five Pillars of the faith were given to the faithful by the Qur'an and Muhammad. They outline the five key practices that Muslims must do.

First pillar: bearing witness (*shahadah* in Arabic)
All Muslims are to bear witness that "there is no God but Allah, and Muhammad is his prophet, his messenger, the one he has sent."

Second pillar: prayer (*salat* in Arabic)
Five times each day, Muslims must pray and prostrate themselves before God: in the morning at dawn; at noon; in the middle of the afternoon; at sunset; and in the evening. They must be pure and clean to pray. This is why a believer washes certain parts of the body before prayer. Praying is always said facing Mecca. From high up in the mosque's minaret, the muezzin calls the faithful to prayer, including communal prayer on Friday, which is a public holiday. Nowadays, the muezzin is often replaced by a loudspeaker.

Third pillar: almsgiving (*zakat* in Arabic)
This is a kind of religious tax. All Muslims must support the community financially. If they can, they are to give 5% or even 10% of their salary to help those who are poor and in need.

Fourth pillar: fasting (*sawn* in Arabic)

Like Christians, Muslims fast. Fasting takes place during the lunar month of Ramadan. Muslims follow the lunar calendar, not the Christians' Gregorian calendar or the Jewish calendar. That's why Ramadan can be at any time of the year.

Fifth pillar: pilgrimage (*hajj* in Arabic)

The pilgrimage takes place during the last month of the lunar year. Whoever does the pilgrimage is obeying the Qur'an, which says, "we made the House a place of assembly and a sanctuary for mankind. Make the place where Abraham stood a place of worship" (*sura* 2:125).

Do Muslims go to heaven after they die?

Yes, of course! Like Jews and Christians, Muslims believe in heaven. They also believe in angels. And they believe in the Last Judgment, after which good people go to heaven and evil people go to hell.

The Qur'an describes heaven and hell like this:
"Heaven has rivers of unpolluted water,
and rivers of fresh milk,
and rivers of wine – delicious for the drinkers –
and rivers of strained honey.
They have all kinds of fruits there,
and forgiveness from their Lord.
Are they similar to those who live forever in the hellfire,
and drink hellish water
that tears up their intestines?"
(*Sura* 46:15)

Chapter 3

DAILY LIFE

Every day of their lives, Jewish, Christian and Muslim
believers place themselves under God's watchful eye in
order to follow his commandments.

How does a person become Jewish?

People are usually born Jewish. A child is considered Jewish if his or her mother is Jewish.

You might think that this is about blood. But it's actually more about milk!

Many people, especially psychologists, see the mother as the "soil" in which the child takes root. From birth, an infant soaks up the "little world" around them along with their mothers' milk. This little world consists of language, the joys and challenges of life, traditions and, of course, religion. This is why the first three years are so important. Later, the child goes to school and leaves the mother's side. Now the role of the father comes more into play. He opens the child to the world and its laws. For Jews, the mother is the one who hands on the faith, because she is truly the "fertile soil" that is needed to make the seed of the little adult grow.

A person can also become a Jew by converting. This means believing in God, observing the commandments of the Torah, and belonging to the people of Israel. Converts are plunged into a ritual bath, the *mikveh*, and the men are circumcised.

What is **circumcision**?

Circumcision is a minor operation that is done on boys. It involves surgically removing the foreskin that covers the end of the penis. This act goes back to Antiquity and was commonly done in the Orient. It is still done today, in North America and other parts of the world.

For Jews, circumcision is the sign of the covenant between God and his people. This mark in the flesh means "I belong to the family of Abraham, to the people of Israel." Today it is almost a "religious identity card": all Jews, even those who are less religiously observant, are circumcised. The ceremony takes place when the child is eight days old, in the home, sometimes in the synagogue, or even in the hospital where the baby was born. The newborn is placed on the knees of his grandfather or another person the family wants to honour. It isn't the rabbi who performs the operation but the *mohel*, who is trained to do it quickly and cleanly. Prayers and blessings join with the cries of the infant, who receives his Hebrew name on this day.

Circumcision reminds a Jewish man that he was not created perfect (like that foreskin, which is a minor imperfection), and that he must perfect himself through deeds and prayers. The Bible often stresses that true circumcision is of the heart.

WHAT ABOUT GIRLS?

Girls are not circumcised, of course. But a month after their birth, they receive their Hebrew name during a blessing in the home.

Is the **rabbi** a **priest** for Jews?

No. The rabbi is a doctor of the Law, a master of the Torah and of the Jewish tradition. His knowledge allows him to try to respond to the thousand and one questions about life and to help believers make decisions about what fits the rules and what does not. People spend five years studying in a rabbinical school before becoming a rabbi.

Rabbi *means "Master" in Hebrew. Jesus was often called "Rabbi."*

The rabbi, who is often a married man, is in charge of a community formed around a synagogue. But he can also teach at a school, visit the sick in the hospital, or be a prison chaplain or the leader of a Scout troop. In some Jewish traditions, women are also rabbis.

The rabbi organizes religious life at the synagogue, but he is not the head of it. Another member of the community has that role. For religious services, the rabbi's presence is not absolutely required because any Jew can lead a religious service as long as at least ten men are present. This group is called a *minyan*, or quorum.

Among rabbis there is no hierarchy. The Chief Rabbi is not the boss of the other rabbis. His title shows that he is honoured for his great wisdom.

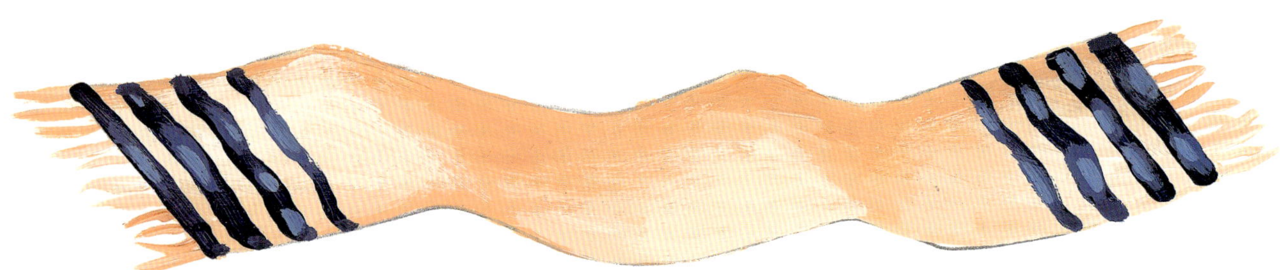

What does it mean to have a **bar mitzvah**?

The *bar mitzvah* is the ceremony by which a boy reaches religious maturity. He is invited to lead a righteous life before God.

At age thirteen he is ready to become *bar mitzvah* – Hebrew for "son of the commandment." From now on, the boy will perform his religious duties (*mitzvot* in Hebrew), such as praying and fasting. On this day, the father stops being responsible for the sins of his son. His son is now an adult in the eyes of God and a full member of the community of Israel.

The ceremony takes place on the Sabbath (Saturday) after the boy's birthday. On that morning, in the synagogue, he will wear a rectangular shawl with fringes at each corner, the *tallit*, for the first time. Men wear this shawl during prayers. Afterwards, there is a big celebration!

The boy gets ready for his bar mitzvah with the help of a scholar. During the ceremony, he must read an excerpt from the Torah in Hebrew. Since Hebrew is a language written without vowels, reading it involves special training.

WHAT ABOUT GIRLS?

Girls reach religious maturity at the age of twelve years and one day. For centuries, there was no ceremony to mark their entry into adulthood. Today, if they wish, girls may study to become *bat mitzvah*, Hebrew for "daughter of the commandment." Like the boys, they can have a party to celebrate this special day.

Why don't Jews eat pork?

It's true that Jews don't eat pork, but pig is not the only animal they are not allowed to eat. Horsemeat, shrimp, and some other foods are also forbidden.

According to the Bible, some animals are clean and others are unclean. The Book of Leviticus reviews the whole of Noah's ark: "From among all the land animals, these are the creatures that you may eat. Any animal that has divided hoofs and is cleft-footed and chews the cud – such you may eat. You shall not eat the following: the camel, for even though it chews the cud, it does not have divided hoofs; it is unclean for you. The hare, for even though it chews the cud, it does not have divided hoofs; it is unclean for you. The pig, for even though it has divided hoofs and is cleft-footed, it does not chew the cud; it is unclean for you" (Leviticus 11:1-8). And the list goes on ...

So it is a matter of animals with divided hoofs and animals that chew their cud. That must mean something! But God doesn't explain, and the Bible doesn't either. And so the wise men of Israel tried to shed some light on the matter.

The divided hoof is the symbol of the two paths that humans are free to choose at any moment in life: the path of good and the path of evil. People need to chew on something, or ruminate (which also means "think about"), if they are to grow in wisdom. A person has to chew on, review and memorize the Word of God, which is food for the heart. In the same way, the person has to chew on, discern and examine what is evil in their life so they can reject it and spit it out.

An animal that does not chew its cud does not bother to examine itself wisely, and an animal with divided hoofs is like a path without direction. Both are declared unclean because they move away from God.

WHAT DOES KOSHER MEAN?

Kosher means "fit" in Hebrew. When it comes to food, kosher means it is suitable for humans to eat. *Kosher* is the term used by Jews, and *halal* ("permissible" in Arabic) is the word Muslims use. These terms are sometimes found on the signs over butcher shops.

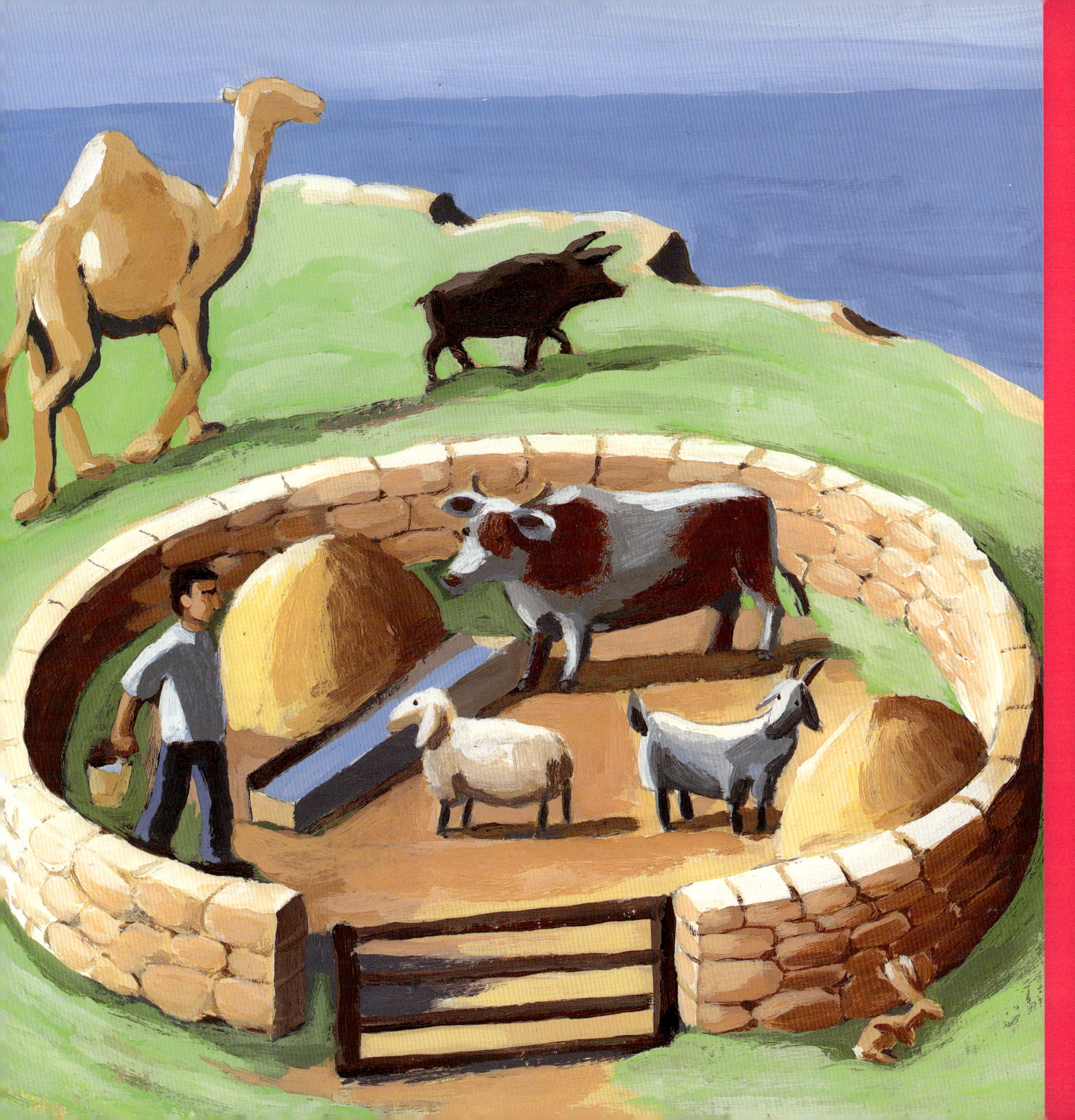

Do the Jews have saints?

Yes. Sanctity, or holiness, is an ideal in life. God himself invites each believer to become holy: "You shall be holy, for I, the Lord your God, am holy" (Leviticus 19:2).

Kadosh is the Hebrew word for "holy." It means "separated." To be holy is to be different, set apart, to stand out from the crowd.

Here is the recipe for becoming holy. The wise men of Israel say, "Just as God is good, you be good; just as God is generous, you be generous." The list is long because God, the source of everything, is infinite. Everyone must draw from this source to become a small reflection of God. To be holy is to be a "mirror of God." It is also to be faithful to the Word of God, the Torah, so that one may in turn become a "living Torah."

But Jews do not have saints in the way that Christians usually understand the term. Jewish saints are not listed on an official calendar. Rabbis do not bestow the title of saint, because only God, who is and remains the source of all holiness, can probe the heart, ponder and reward those who live holy and faithful lives. But this doesn't stop some believers from going to pray at the graves of people whose lives were marked by goodness and faith in God. So the rabbis remind people that prayers are not to be addressed to the person, but always to God, in memory of the person's good deeds.

VISITING A SAINT'S GRAVE

Making a pilgrimage to a saint's grave is not really a Jewish custom. One scholar even said that it is not necessary to put up tombstones for saints, because their words and actions are enough to make sure their memory lives on. But this custom does exist, because of the influence of Christians and Muslims. People light candles at the grave and leave wishes written out on small pieces of paper.

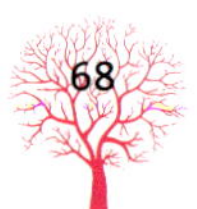

Why don't some commandments apply to Jewish women?

Unlike men, Jewish women do not wear the prayer shawl, and at the synagogue, they are kept separate and do not participate a lot in the liturgy. In Judaism, it can seem that women are token members.

But the Jewish religion is not only lived in the synagogue; it is lived even more within the home. There, everything falls to the woman. Not just the daily housework – that would be too easy! The woman's role is to make the home radiate with a welcoming spirit, a pleasant atmosphere, and children who have been raised well, of course, but also, under God's watchful eye, meals that respect the dietary laws. All this takes time, but it is time given to God. This is why women are excused from some of the commandments. Their lives witness to God's love in a different way.

Things are changing now. Girls celebrate their religious maturity at the age of twelve. Women are called to read from the Torah, some are lawyers on rabbinical tribunals, and some become rabbis. These changes in attitudes are not accepted everywhere. They vary from one country to another.

Why do you have to be baptized to become a Christian?

You can admire Jesus or enjoy reading the Gospels without being baptized. But no one can become a Christian without the sacrament of baptism. This action brings a person into the family of Jesus' disciples, the Church. This doesn't mean that you are a "good" Christian just because you have been baptized! The most important thing is not to have a baptismal certificate, but to have faith.

To baptize comes from the Greek word baptizo, which means to "immerse." The future Christian is immersed in the life and death of the risen Christ.

A person can be baptized at any age. When babies are to be baptized (which is when most people receive the sacrament), it is the parents who prepare themselves for the celebration and who proclaim their faith on behalf of the child. Older children who ask for baptism, if their parents agree, will prepare by going through a type of instruction called catechesis, in which they learn about the Bible and the Christian faith. Many adults, after discovering Christ, also ask for baptism. They may spend years preparing for it. Children and adults who are preparing for baptism are called catechumens.

During the celebration of baptism, the priest pours a stream of water over the head of the new Christian and says, "I baptize you in the name of the Father, and of the Son, and of the Holy Spirit." Long ago, baptism was done by immersion: the person was completely immersed in water. The Orthodox and some other Christian churches still baptize people by immersion.

To be Christian is to believe that Jesus is truly the Son of God, who became human and died for us so that we may have life, even after death. This means that, for a Christian, Jesus is not simply some famous person from the past (like the Buddha, Socrates or Confucius), but is alive today – and that they can have the same relationship with him as they have with a teacher or a friend. They can speak to him, feel his mysterious presence, and listen to his word through the Bible texts, in the events of daily life, or in the silence of their heart.

Do **Catholics**, **Protestants** and **Orthodox** have the **same** baptism?

Yes, exactly the same, and that's very important. It means they are all Christians. They share the same faith in God and in Jesus Christ. What unites them is much more important than what divides them in how they express their beliefs or practise their faith.

This is why, when a Christian leaves one church to join another (for example, a Catholic becomes Protestant, or an Anglican becomes Orthodox), the person is not baptized again in the new community.

As Saint Paul said, for all Christians there is only one baptism, because they share the same faith in the same Lord (Jesus) and in the same God (the Father).

What is a **sacrament**?

The word "sacrament" is a bit complicated. In Greek it means "mystery." But it also has a connection to the word "sacred" because God is part of it. A sacrament is an action by which believers receive a special grace or gift from God to help them live as God asks.

In a sacrament, the action does what the words that go with it have proclaimed. For example, in the sacrament of reconciliation, the priest speaks on behalf of God. The priest says to the person who has come to confess his sins and be forgiven, "I absolve you of your sins," and the person is truly forgiven by God!

All Christians recognize baptism and eucharist as sacraments, because Jesus himself wanted people to experience them. He told his disciples to go to the ends of the earth to baptize, and he told them at the Last Supper to continue to share the bread and wine as he had done. These had become his body and blood, given to save humanity. For Protestants, there are no other sacraments besides baptism and eucharist.

Catholics and Orthodox recognize five other sacraments: confirmation (a person receives the Holy Spirit to have the strength to be a disciple of Jesus); reconciliation (a person's sins are forgiven); marriage (a man and a woman join their lives together before God), holy orders (a man dedicates himself as a deacon, priest or bishop to carry out a mission in the name of the Church); and the sacrament of the sick (a person receives the strength they need to deal with illness).

How does a person become a saint?

Saints are people who, everyone agrees, lived close to God, in the very image of Jesus. Saints are not heroes or superheroes, but people who put God first in their life and let God lead them along paths that were sometimes unexpected.

Some saints had an extraordinary destiny, like Joan of Arc, the young shepherdess whom God called to liberate France, or the many martyrs who died for their faith, such as Maximilian Kolbe, a priest who died in a concentration camp during the Second World War. Others led lives that were less dramatic but were dedicated to God and to others, like Thérèse of Lisieux in her convent in France or Kateri Tekakwitha who lived in the 1600s in North America.

To recognize a person's holiness, the Catholic Church does an in-depth investigation. Next, the Church declares the person "blessed" (this is called beatification), and then a "saint" (this is called canonization). Since the twelfth century, only the pope can beatify and canonize a Christian.

All recognized saints (and there are thousands of them) are listed in the Church's official calendar. But thousands more saints who lived good lives that others can imitate are not found in that calendar. All Christians are invited by their baptism to be saints – to imitate the holiness of Christ by leading good and holy lives.

What's the difference between a priest and a monk?

There are several ways to give one's life to God and the Church. These include becoming a priest (for Catholics, this is for men only) or entering religious life. Religious life is open to women as well as men. Religious men and women live in separate communities.

Religious life is divided into two families. Some choose apostolic life, living in the world and working alongside others. And some choose contemplative life, praying and working inside a monastery – the men are called "monks" and the women are called "nuns."

There are two types of priests. Most are diocesan or secular priests who serve the Church in a certain area called a diocese. Religious priests, like the members of religious communities, follow a "rule of life." A priest can be a monk, but not all monks are priests. Monks who are not priests are known as "brothers."

Why do **Catholics** eat **fish** on **Fridays**?

This is an ancient tradition in the Church, not something that Christ asked people to do. In the past, the Church required the faithful not to eat meat on Fridays because Jesus died on a Friday. The people had to do penance on this day to join with the suffering of his Passion. Most people relied on meat in their diet: to go without it, or "to abstain" from it, was an act of self-denial.

For the same reason, Catholics used to abstain from eating meat during Lent, a season in which the faithful are invited to prepare themselves for the joy of Easter. They would also avoid meat on the eve of important feasts. Since meat was not allowed, and people still needed to keep up their strength, Christians began to eat fish. This meal, being more humble, was seen as more appropriate.

This rule has been simplified over time: Catholics are now asked not to eat meat on Ash Wednesday, the Fridays in Lent, and Good Friday.

Why are there **different** **Protestant** churches?

Christians form a large family, with many different branches and a countless number of small offshoots. They all share the same faith and acknowledge the same baptism. Jesus asked that they always be one, united. Over the centuries, there were arguments among groups of Christians. Unfortunately, these led to divisions, especially among Catholics, Protestants and Orthodox!

There are many Protestant churches because Protestants are less concerned about church structures than Catholics and Orthodox are. Some of the Protestant churches are very large, such as the Lutherans (named after Martin Luther, who started a movement in the sixteenth century by "protesting" against the Vatican, which gave us the word "Protestant"); Reformed (also called Calvinists, named after John Calvin, a great reformer of the Church at that time); and Baptists. Many small groups are always coming into being, either to be closer to a country or region's way of thinking, or to shake up the bigger churches to remind them of their mission. Movements of spiritual awakening appear regularly. One of the most recent is the charismatic renewal: it emerged among Protestants in the United States but also developed among Catholics in Europe.

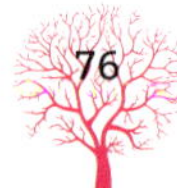

How do you become a **priest** or a **pastor**?

Being a priest or pastor is not like any other "job." It involves dedicating your life to serving Christians in a parish, a chaplaincy, or a church movement and proclaiming the Gospel to those who haven't heard it. You don't have to be a "super-Christian," but you do have to put God and other people first in your life.

For Catholics and Orthodox, being a priest is a lifelong commitment that is reserved for men only. Catholic priests are not allowed to marry. Protestant men and women, married or single, can be pastors, but their commitment is not necessarily for life. One of the most important tasks for pastors is to explain the Word of God during the liturgy. In all cases, this means a long period of study (around six years) to become very familiar with the Bible and the fundamentals of the Christian faith.

WHO CREATED THE OFFICE OF THE POPE?

Catholics begin with the words of Jesus himself. Jesus asked Peter to be the leader of the disciples: "You are Peter and upon this rock I will build my church." Since Peter died in Rome, the bishop of that city received the title of "pope," which means "father" in Greek. So it was not Jesus who directly created the office of the pope; but the role of the pope matches what Jesus wanted so that the Church would be organized at the global level. That's why the pope lives in Rome and goes out to visit Catholic communities to encourage and strengthen them.

Why don't **Muslims** eat in the daytime during **Ramadan**?

During the month of Ramadan, Muslims practise fasting, just as Christians do on certain days in Lent. According to the rules in the Qur'an, Muslims are required to abstain from eating from sunrise, when "one is able distinguish a white thread from a black thread," until sunset. This gives Muslims more time to worship God.

Why are Muslims not allowed to eat pork and drink alcohol?

It has more to do with ritual than with law. The problem is that, at the time of the Prophet, pork was thought to cause illness. Since meat could not be preserved, it could not be eaten in the desert where the air was very hot and the meat would go bad quickly. Also, it was prohibited to eat meat from a dead animal that had not been drained of its blood before being butchered. Alcohol is forbidden because it can cause serious problems in people's lives. That's why Muhammad told people to stay away from alcohol and especially not to pray if they were drunk. Later he preached against drinking alcohol for health reasons rather than religious ones.

Today, Muslim tradition still forbids pork and alcohol, even though hygiene and social customs have changed.

What is an **imam**?

In Arabic, the word *imam* means "in front." For most of the world's Muslims, the imam is a prayer leader. He is chosen by the community, but he is not a cleric like a Catholic priest is. Still, he must be recognized for his piety and his knowledge about liturgy (prayer rituals) to make sure that the rites are done correctly and prayer happens regularly. The community can decide to choose a new imam at any time.

The imam must look after the mosque, of course, but the high point of the week is communal prayer on Friday. At this time, the imam preaches the *khutbah*, or sermon. It can be on a religious, political or moral topic. He addresses the faithful from a raised pulpit that is part of the ritual furnishings of the mosque. The imam is thus the master of ceremonies, and, as his title would suggest, he stands at the front to lead the prayer.

HOW DOES SOMEONE BECOME AN IMAM?

A man becomes an imam when the community recognizes him as someone who is worthy of being imitated, who has moral authority, and who is very familiar with the prayers and can explain the Qur'an to the faithful.

Do **Muslims** have **saints**?

No, Muslims do not have saints. In Islam, no one stands between God and humanity. This is the uniqueness of Islam. Those who have knowledge, said the Prophet, have the right to interpret, but not to speak in the name of Islam or Muslims.

Certain countries, however, do have mausoleums of men who were well respected and serve as role models because of the lives they led. This is why people in Western countries sometimes mistakenly thought that Muslims believed these men to be saints.

Do Muslims have a pope?

No. Because Islam does not recognize any intermediaries between the believer and the Creator, there is no pope.

But it is true that the caliph acted in some ways as a pope for the Muslims, because he was the leader of the faithful. The caliphate had both spiritual and earthly power, which was often given to the grand vizier – a kind of prime minister.

For a very long time, the caliph was always being challenged. The caliphate of Baghdad was contested by the Ottomans (today, the Turks) in the thirteenth century, and so it passed from Medina, at the beginning of Islam, to Damascus in 661, then to Baghdad, and finally to Istanbul after the capture of Constantinople by the Ottomans in 1453.

The caliphate was abolished in 1924. Since then, Muslims feel a little like caliphate orphans. Today, Islamists (see page 28) of various schools of thought, whether they be the Gulen Movement (Turkish Islam), the Muslim Brotherhood or the Tabligh Movement, want the caliphate to be restored so Muslims can once again be part of the *umma* – one Muslim community, without boundaries.

Why do some Muslim women wear a headscarf?

It's a tradition. The Qur'an does not say a single word about hair, but it says that female Muslims – the wives of the Prophet and the wives of believers – are required to "to cover up their adornments." The female faithful were also required to wear a veil, especially the wives of the prophet Muhammad, because it was customary in his tribe and later among his companions to demand that the female faithful avoid the lustful stares of men. For the same reason, women had to wear a *jellaba* (a long outer robe with full sleeves) that went from the neck to the feet.

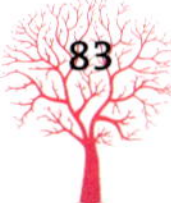

How do Jews get married?

For Jews, marriage is a divine commandment, present from the time of Creation with Adam and Eve. Marriage is a gift that God gives to men and women so they can be closer to him.

The ceremony often takes place in the synagogue, but it can also happen outdoors.

When the rabbi greets the bride and groom, he compares their love to God's love, because God made a covenant with humanity. In the same way, the couple makes a covenant to be faithful to one another. The rabbi prays the first blessing over the wine, a sign of joy. The couple drinks from the same glass. Then the groom slides a ring onto the bride's index finger. When she bends her finger, she is saying "yes." A few cheers burst forth from the assembly. The *ketubah*, or marriage contract, is then read. The man welcomes the woman under the prayer shawl, for they are now husband and wife. At the end of the ceremony, the husband breaks a glass with his heel as a sign of sadness in memory of the destruction of the Temple of Jerusalem.

It is permitted for Jews to dissolve an unhappy marriage. Either the man or the woman can ask for a divorce, but both must agree. The rabbinical tribunal reads the letter of divorce. The man and woman can later marry someone else.

CHUPPAH

The *chuppah* is the wedding canopy under which the couple gets married. It represents the new home the couple will make together, one that is always welcoming. Hospitality is an important duty in Judaism, and the *chuppah* is a reminder of Abraham's tent, which was open "to the four winds," to guests and strangers alike.

How do **Christians** get **married**?

For Christians, marriage between a man and a woman is the image of God's covenant with all humanity. It is a celebration of the love between two persons and the love of God for all people. This is why the Church insists that Christian couples marry freely, promise lifelong fidelity, and have the desire to start a family. On behalf of the Church, the priest or pastor receives this commitment that the couple is making before God.

The ceremony is very joyful. The most important moment is when the bride and groom exchange their marriage vows. By this gesture, they publicly choose each other as husband and wife and promise to be faithful to each other. As a sign of this commitment, each gives the other a ring that will remind them each day of the promise they have just made.

At Catholic weddings, the priest says special prayers for the newlyweds before blessing their union. For the Orthodox, the priest burns incense and waves the smoke over the couple and places a golden crown on each of their heads to recall the "royal" covenant between Christ and the Church. Then he dances with them around the icons. At Protestant weddings, the pastor gives a Bible to the bride and groom. The newlyweds, along with the witnesses they have chosen, then sign the register that will be an official record of this wonderful day.

Can Christians **divorce**?

That depends on which Christian church you belong to. The Catholic Church does not allow divorce, because marriage, for Catholics, is a symbol of God's love for humanity. God cannot break a covenant with us!

A Catholic couple can end their civil marriage, but not their sacramental marriage. Catholics can be married in the Church again if their previous marriage is annulled by the Church.

The Orthodox accept that a marriage can fail. Couples can divorce and get married again in the Church to someone else. A person is allowed to marry in the Church two times only. A second marriage is celebrated much more simply.

Protestants, for whom marriage is not a sacrament, accept that a remarriage held at city hall can be recognized by the Church as a new union in God's eyes.

How do Muslims get married?

To marry is an obligation for Muslims. Neither the Qur'an nor the tradition (the *Sunna*) encourages people to stay single. But marriage is encouraged, glorified and pleasing to God. "Your wives are your fields. Go, then, into your fields as you will," says the Qur'an (*sura* 2, verse 223).

Unlike Catholics and Orthodox , Muslims do not see marriage as a sacrament but simply as a contract. This contract is between the bride and groom and between the two families. It provides for all cases of divorce, repudiation and the care of children. The contract is meant to cover everything. But sometimes the contract is not well written. For example, when people from a small village who have little education prepare a marriage contract for their fourteen- or fifteen-year-old daughter, it may not be complete. Later, if there is a divorce or repudiation, the wife may find herself in a difficult situation.

The marriage contract is concluded before an Islamic judge, called a *qadi*, who signs the document.

A Muslim may have up to four lawful wives as long as he treats and honours them equally. Polygamy is allowed in Islam, but it has become less common in recent years. Some countries have laws against it.

CAN MUSLIMS DIVORCE?

Yes, Muslims can divorce. Either the man or the woman can ask for a divorce. The man can also repudiate (reject) his wife for reasons that may seem minor. All he has to do is repeat the word *talaq*, which means "I divorce you," three times so that the repudiation will be recognized by the community.

What happens at Jewish funerals?

When a Jewish person dies, the body is carefully washed. This respectful ritual is done to take away any impurities: the hair and nails are cut, and the body is sprinkled with water and perfumed. No clothing or jewellery adorns the body, because it is written in the Book of Ecclesiastes: "As they came from their mother's womb, so they shall go again, naked as they came" (5:15). The body is covered with a white sheet. A prayer shawl with the fringes cut off is placed on men's bodies. The body is then placed on some straw on the ground, with a candle near the head to symbolize that the soul is still living. The burial takes place as soon as possible.

In most cases, there is no special ceremony at the synagogue. Prayers are said at the cemetery, where there are no flowers or wreaths. Once the coffin is placed in the grave, the rabbi throws three shovelfuls of earth on it. The other people who are there do the same, and then family members tear a part of their clothing to show their sadness. For one year, a light shines in the home in memory of the person who has died.

CREMATION

In Judaism, cremation of the body is forbidden because the body, like the soul, belongs to God. One returns to dust, not to ashes! The Jewish community is divided when it comes to organ donation. For some people, the body must not be mutilated. For others, such generosity is permitted because to save a life is a divine duty.

What happens at **Christian funerals**?

A funeral is sad, of course, but it is also a time of hope. For Christians, death is not the end of life, since Jesus rose from the dead. Church funerals express this strong belief that goes beyond the pain we feel when someone we love dies.

At the funeral, people read aloud from Bible texts that speak of faith in the resurrection of the dead – not only of Christ, but of all those who came after him who have lived in the spirit of his Gospel. A priest presides at the ceremony (today, trained laypeople may also take on this role).

Christians pray that God will welcome the deceased, and they express their desire to see their loved one again someday. The coffin is then sprinkled with holy water, to recall baptism, before the priest incenses the body as a sign of respect. After the ceremony in the church, the people accompany the deceased person to the cemetery to hear a final prayer of farewell beside the grave where the body will be buried.

CHRISTIANS AND CREMATION

For a long time, the Church did not accept cremation, because in the Gospels, the body is compared to a seed that must be buried in the soil in order to bear fruit. Today, many Christians wish to be cremated for a variety of reasons. The Church is no longer opposed to cremation, as long as the person has expressed their faith in the resurrection of the dead.

After death, will Christians be raised to new life?

Yes. It is part of the Christian faith to believe in the resurrection of the dead. That is why God began by raising Jesus from the dead.

Catholics and Orthodox tend to use different images for the resurrection. Catholic art shows Jesus alive as he leaves his tomb and appears to his friends. Orthodox art portrays him descending into "hell" (the place of the dead) to draw Adam, Eve and all humanity out with him. This is a way of saying that, because Christ rose from the dead, Christians can no longer say someone is dead forever: one day the person will experience new life – eternal life – with God.

But is resurrection only for Christians? Not at all! In chapter 25 of his Gospel, Matthew says that, at the end of time, all people will be judged on what they have done. Eternal life, says Jesus, is for all who have done good things for those around them, especially the hungry, the sick and strangers. Without even knowing it, they have served Christ by caring for those in need.

HELL

The underworld, or hell, is the resting place of all who have died since the creation of the world. The word comes from the Latin word *infernus*, meaning "that which is below." The Old Testament speaks of *Sheol* to describe the place of the dead. The New Testament uses the word "hell" to mean "separated from God."

What happens at **Muslim funerals**?

Muslim funeral rites are a little different from one country to another, but the key parts are found in the law. These start with the funeral wake around the body, with the family and the imam present. The imam reads and recites certain prayers, along with some verses from the Qur'an. The body is completely washed and covered with a simple white sheet. People say a prayer as they leave the deceased's home or the hospital, and then the body is buried in a coffin with the face toward Mecca. The use of tombstones or burial vaults is not a Muslim tradition.

Do MUSLIMS ALLOW CREMATION?
Cremation and mummification are forbidden by Islamic law. They are considered to be a kind of provocation and desecration of the body. Suicide is also forbidden.

Chapter 4

PRAYERS AND RELIGIOUS PRACTICES

To please God and to speak to God, Jews, Christians
and Muslims do many things that reflect their faith.

What is **prayer**?

Prayer is the most religious thing people can do, because when they pray, they are talking to God. Religion is not first of all a collection of doctrines or instructions you have to accept or binding rituals you have to do. Above all, it is a living relationship, a connection between a person and God.

We can speak to God in all kinds of ways using many kinds of prayers. There are prayers of praise, where we say how happy we are about everything that is, beginning with God and us; prayers of petition, where we ask God for what we think we need; prayers of thanksgiving, where we thank God for all he has given us so we can live, such as our family, friends, good experiences, and even requests he has granted to us; and prayers of intercession, where we place in God's care the people we love or the things that worry us.

No one is forced to pray. Prayer is an activity that comes from the heart. Prayer seems natural from the moment God becomes a living God or the believer. The believer recognizes that God is the Creator and that God loves his creature.

In all religions, prayer is essential for the faithful, whether they are alone or gathered with the community. You can pray with your own words and gestures, standing, sitting, kneeling or with your hands raised to heaven. You can speak to God in a loud voice or in the silence of your heart. You can say your religion's formal prayers that you have learned by heart. In this way you can join with other believers who share the same faith as you.

What are the great Jewish prayers?

The faithful Jew loves to pray, and may bless God a hundred times a day! That desire to pray has marked the entire history of the people of Israel, and they are sometimes called "the people of prayer."

The great prayer is the *Shema Israel*, which means "Hear, O Israel" in Hebrew. It is found in the Book of Deuteronomy (6:4-9). It begins with these words: "Hear, O Israel, the Lord is our God, the Lord is one. You shall love the Lord your God with all your heart and with all your soul and with all your strength." The *Shema* sums up the Jewish faith: God is one, and he has made a covenant with his people. Learned at a very early age and recited during the morning and evening, it accompanies believers throughout life until their final breath.

The other great prayer is the *kaddish*, which exalts and sings about the Name of the Lord. It begins with these words: "May his great name be exalted and sanctified." In this prayer, Jews express their desire for the Kingdom of God on earth. The *kaddish* is the source of the Our Father, the great Christian prayer.

Jewish prayer is also a continual blessing that gives thanks to God for each moment of life. Everything comes from God. So, before a meal or when gazing at a beautiful landscape, the faithful bless God, saying, "You are blessed, Lord our God, King of the world."

What are the great Christian prayers?

Christians like to use certain Jewish prayers, such as the psalms and canticles of the Old Testament. But they mostly pray with their own words, often inspired by the Gospel.

The greatest Christian prayer is the **Our Father**, because Jesus himself taught it to his disciples when they asked him to teach them how to pray:

> Our Father, who art in heaven,
>
> hallowed be thy name;
>
> thy kingdom come,
>
> thy will be done
>
> on earth as it is in heaven.
>
> Give us this day our daily bread,
>
> and forgive us our trespasses,
>
> as we forgive those who trespass against us;
>
> and lead us not into temptation,
>
> but deliver us from evil.

The Orthodox love the **Jesus Prayer**, which is very short: "Lord Jesus Christ, Son of God, have mercy on me, a sinner." Some of the faithful recite it continually to the rhythm of their breathing!

Catholics not only pray to God the Father or to Jesus, but also ask the saints to pray to God for them. The best-known example is the Hail Mary, a prayer to the Blessed Virgin, the mother of Jesus. Many people recite it over and over when they pray the rosary. Another prayer is the Magnificat, a Latin word that means "magnify." The evangelist Luke tells us that the Virgin Mary sang this prayer of praise when her cousin Elizabeth greeted her when Mary was pregnant with Jesus.

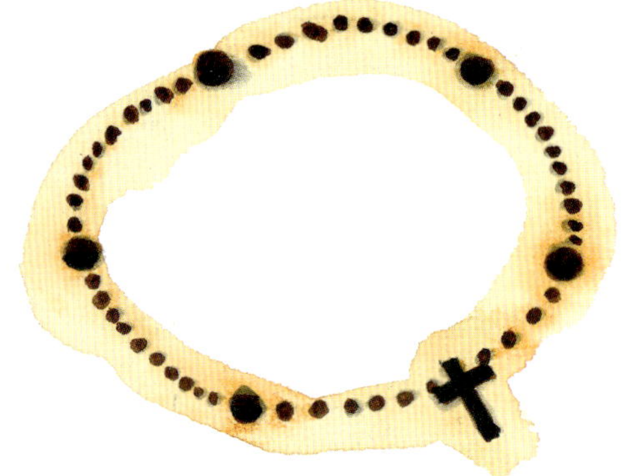

What are the great Muslim prayers?

Muslim prayers are prayers the faithful must say every day to give thanks to God. These tend to be passages from the Qur'an.

To mark certain events in life, like birth and especially death, Muslims say special prayers, offering to God the life of the newborn or the person who has died and asking God to guide the newborn on earth and the deceased in the afterlife.

What is a **synagogue**?

"Synagogue" comes from the Greek word meaning "assembly." In Hebrew it is called *beit knesset*, meaning "house of assembly." For Jews this is an ideal meeting place for prayer, feasts and studying the Torah.

The synagogue dates from the sixth century B.C. At that time, the Hebrews were living in exile in Babylon, far from Jerusalem, cut off from their Temple. They felt the need to be with one another so they could study the Word of God together. This need gave birth to the synagogue.

A few centuries later, in A.D. 70, when the Temple of Jerusalem, the only place of worship for the Jews, was destroyed, the synagogue became the new house of prayer. On the back wall is a cabinet, the Holy Ark, which contains the Torah scrolls. In the centre is an elevated platform, the *bimah*, which has a table for reading from these scrolls.

"ORIENTED" HOUSES OF PRAYER

Believers place great importance on how their places of prayer are built. Jewish synagogues face Jerusalem, where the Temple, the dwelling place of God, was built.

Christian churches point to the east, in the direction of the rising sun (the Orient), the image of the risen Christ.

Mosques face Mecca, the holy city of Islam.

Why do **Jewish men** wear a small **skullcap** when they pray?

This small skullcap is called a *kippah*. Jews like to wear it so they will never forget that God is above them. It reminds them that they are infinitely small before the Creator.

The *kippah* is not a religious object. It is a simple head covering. Any hat will do. Wearing a *kippah* is becoming more common, because for those who wear it all day, it is smaller, lighter and cooler. Men must wear it in the synagogue. Women do not wear a *kippah*, but they, too, must cover their heads when they come to the synagogue, out of respect for God and because hair is considered very seductive. Anything may be used to conceal it: a hat, scarf, bonnet, hood, even a wig!

Another garment unique to Jewish prayer is the *tallit*. It is a white or natural-coloured shawl, decorated with fringes at the four corners. These fringes are called *tzitzit* and they symbolize God's commandments. Men wear the *tallit* especially during morning prayer and on the Sabbath. Worn from the head to the shoulders, it is like a small tent under which it is easy to meditate. In this private spot, the believer can turn his heart to the Creator. The blue stripe that highlights the *tallit* is also the colour of the sky, the colour of God.

What is **church**?

"Church" comes from the Greek word meaning "assembly." Before it was used to describe the building where Christians gather, the term referred to the people who gather.

We write "Church" with a capital "C" to describe the assembly of believers, while "church" with a small "c" refers to the building where they gather.

These Christian places of worship (which some Protestants call "temples") can be all different sizes, from a small chapel in a rural area to a huge cathedral, the church of the bishop, in a big city. But all of these buildings are there to allow the disciples of Jesus to come and pray, alone or with others, and to celebrate high points in the Christian life, such as the Mass, baptisms, weddings and funerals. Going to church for these celebrations is a way of placing one's whole existence in the sight of God.

Churches almost always form a cross shape. The longest part, the nave, is where the faithful sit. This area is extended in the front by a shorter, rounded space called the sanctuary. The altar (see page 105) is there, along with the priest and altar servers during Mass. An area that crosses the nave near the front of the church is called the transept. It sometimes includes separate small chapels.

Catholic churches tend to be ornate, with paintings and statues of saints. Light enters through colourful stained glass windows that contain scenes from the Bible and the lives of the saints.

Protestant churches are plainer. For Protestants, the most important thing is listening to the Word of God. That is why there is always a large open Bible on the altar and a raised pulpit from which the pastor preaches about the Word of God.

Orthodox churches are richly decorated, with frescoes (paintings) on the walls and sacred paintings called icons (see page 109). The sanctuary is separated from the nave by a large wall containing images of saints, called the iconostasis.

What is the big table at the front of the church used for?

This big table is called an altar. The word comes from Latin and means "elevated" (raised). The altar is there especially to honour God. In the Bible, the first believers created stone mounds where God would appear to them. When the Jews had the Temple in Jerusalem, animals were sacrificed on the altar as a way to call upon God.

Christians took up this idea. But for them, the greatest sacrifice ever offered to God was that of his own son, Jesus, who died to save humanity. In churches, the memorial of this sacrifice takes place on the altar during the celebration of the Mass (the eucharist). The priest repeats the actions that Jesus did during the Last Supper with his disciples: he blesses and shares the bread and wine, which become for believers the Body and Blood of Christ.

The altar, which is always in the sanctuary, is either square or rectangular, and is often carved or decorated in some way. It can be made of stone, as if to offer a sacrifice, or of wood, to be a table for a meal.

Why do **Christians** make the sign of the cross before praying?

When Catholics begin and end their prayers, and when they enter a church, they make the sign of the cross on their bodies. They lift their right hand to their forehead, then to their chest, and finally to their shoulders, beginning with the left. As they do this, they say, "In the name of the Father, and of the Son, and of the Holy Spirit. Amen."

The sign of the cross is a reminder that Christian faith rests upon Christ, who was crucified and died to save people from sin and death.

Making the sign of the cross on the body is also a way of saying that one's entire being (body, heart and spirit) is "wrapped" in this mystery.

In general, Protestants do not make the sign of the cross, because they avoid exterior displays of religion. For them, faith is mostly an interior practice. They show their faith by living the Gospel. Still, some Protestants, such as Lutherans, do make the sign of the cross.

Why do Catholics go to Mass on Sunday?

Catholics go to Mass because this is what Jesus asked his disciples to do. During the Last Supper that he shared with his apostles before he died, he took bread and wine, which he blessed and gave to them, saying that it was his body and blood that he was giving up for them. Then he ordered them to do this in memory of him.

After Christ's death and resurrection, the first Christians gathered together to share bread and wine, using the same words and actions as Jesus, to show that his sacrifice is always current. This time of prayer is called the "eucharist," from the Greek word meaning "to give thanks" or "to say thank you." The "Mass" is another word that is used to mean eucharist. This is the most wonderful way to thank God for sending his son Jesus to save humanity from death. That's why it shouldn't be surprising that Catholics go to Mass: this is how they show that they want to take part in what is both the source and summit of their faith life.

People can go to Mass any day of the week. So why go to Mass on Sunday? In Latin, Sunday means "the day of the Lord," because it was on Easter Sunday morning that Jesus was raised from the dead. Since the Mass is the sacrament of life received from God, it makes sense to celebrate it in a special way on that day. Sunday is a day when everyone is called to think about God and to pray more than on the other days of the week.

WHY DO CHURCH BELLS SOMETIMES RING BEFORE MASS?

This is an old tradition that some churches still do today. It is a simple, practical way to let people know that Mass is starting and to remind them of God's presence in the Christian community.

Do **Protestants** go to **Mass**, too?

Protestants do not see the eucharist in exactly the same way Catholics do, and even among themselves they have different ways of thinking about the eucharist and celebrating it.

Protestants call this celebration "the Lord's Supper." This is the name Christians give to the last meal that Christ had with his disciples before being arrested and sentenced to death.

Catholics attach more importance to communion, while Protestants emphasize listening to the Word of God.

For some Protestants, Christ becomes present in a purely symbolic manner in the bread and wine, and communion is mainly a way of expressing the common faith and mission that all people share in the name of Jesus. The role of the pastor is not to preside over the community in Christ's name, but to teach those gathered. Protestants gather on Sunday at church: even if they don't celebrate the Lord's Supper every week, they go there to listen to God's Word and study it. The Word of God is at the centre of their life and faith.

Why do the Orthodox kiss paintings?

These paintings are called "icons" (from the Greek word meaning "image"). Icons are found in all Orthodox churches and in the homes of the faithful.

These images, painted on wooden planks or directly on walls, like frescoes, are often several centuries old. They depict either scenes from the Bible or saints. They are painted according to strict rules. Each scene or person must be depicted following a precise model, and only natural products are used to paint them. That's why the artist who paints icons must go through a long period of training, both artistic and spiritual. The artist prays intensely and fasts when painting.

Icons are very important to the faith of Orthodox believers. They do more than show respect for icons: they also venerate what the icons depict by kissing and decorating them, by incensing and illuminating them with candles, and by bowing and making the sign of the cross before them. God speaks, in a certain way, through these images – not so much by the stories and faces they contain, but by the contemplation that they invite. For the Orthodox, it is not so much the believer who looks upon the icon, but God who gazes at the believer with great love through the icon. These images are a form of God's presence in the midst of believers.

What is a **mosque**?

A mosque is the place of worship for Muslims. Believers go to the mosque to pray to God during communal prayer on Fridays at midday. There is also a sermon by the imam, the man who leads the prayer. He comments on a passage from the Qur'an, the holy book of Islam.

The imam delivers his sermon from a raised pulpit called a *minbar*. It is near an empty alcove, called a *mihrab*, which indicates the *qibla*, the direction of Mecca.

The role of the mosque is also to welcome the poor. Whenever they seek shelter or need to rest somewhere, they can come to the mosque.

The mosque is also a place of instruction, in particular of the Qur'anic school, where young children learn the Qur'an and the words of the Prophet, called the *Haddith*.

WHY DO PEOPLE TAKE OFF THEIR SHOES BEFORE ENTERING A MOSQUE?

Muslims take off their shoes to show respect and to stress the difference between the place where they are now and the place they have just left. In the courtyard of the mosque, there is usually a fountain where Muslims can do their ablutions before entering for prayer. They must wash their hands, arms, feet, face, ears and eyes – in other words, cleanse themselves of what they have seen, heard or touched that could be unclean in their daily life, so they are clean and acceptable to God.

Why do **Muslims** **kneel** to pray?

Muslim prayer is a recitation along with an action that has several important movements. Prayer has three parts. The introduction, which is said while standing, invokes Allah, "the Lord of the Worlds." The prayer itself starts with the recitation of the *fatiha*, the first *sura* of the Qur'an. Then the person bows, with the hands touching the knees, before standing up straight again to recite another prayer. The person then prostrates himself, forehead on the ground, before going onto his knees while reciting more prayers. He ends his prayer, which always contains the words of the *Shahadah* (Creed) and the blessing of the Prophet, seated on his heels.

Why do **Muslims** pray on **Friday?**

For Muslims, Friday prayer is the most important of all prayers. On this day, prayer always includes a sermon by the imam. Also, the prayer is communal: the whole community assembles at the mosque and prays together, giving thanks to God. The Prophet once told his companions that communal prayer is 27 times more valuable than private prayer.

HOW DO MUSLIMS KNOW WHEN IT IS TIME TO PRAY?

Muslims set their prayer times by the position of the sun. Some countries set a specific hour of the day to start praying.

Do Muslims venerate the Virgin Mary?

Yes. Maryam, as Muslims call her, is mentioned 72 times in the Qur'an. She is honoured in this way because she is the mother of Jesus, who is a great prophet in the eyes of Muslims. Jesus, in Arabic, is 'Isa.

This veneration also includes belief in the virginity of Mary. Jesus was born of Mary and the breath of the Spirit. But Muslims do not believe that Jesus was divine or the Son of God. This is why they do not give Mary the title "Mother of God."

Why are **men** and **women** **separated** in a mosque?

For one simple reason: to avoid distracting each other! But Muslims do not just sit separately at the mosque. To respect the instructions and orders of the Prophet, they put up a hijab – a cloth screen – between the men and the women in the prayer hall.

Hijab is also the word for the veil women wear to cover their hair.

Chapter 5

FEASTS AND SYMBOLS

Believers celebrate God's presence in their lives. There are many moments when people can show that God makes them happy.

Why don't Jews, Christians and Muslims use the same calendar?

The sun and the moon, the "two great lights" of the Bible, have allowed us to place ourselves in time. Some peoples chose the moon, while others chose the sun to set time. This choice led to two types of calendars: the lunar calendar and the solar calendar.

The lunar calendar is easy to follow. With each new moon, a new month begins, and the 15th of the month is the full moon. The months last for 29 or 30 days. When we multiply this number by twelve, we end up with a year of 354 or 355 days. But the Earth takes 365 days to travel around the sun …

The solar calendar takes these 365 days into account: the months are a little longer – 30 or 31 days. This small difference of one or two days between the solar and lunar months may seem minor, but over time, this difference gets bigger and bigger and ends up affecting the calendar. In some years, spring could begin in January and Christmas would be in the middle of summer!

To keep the date of feasts in the same season, the Jews adopted the luni-solar calendar. About every three years, they add a thirteenth month to recover the lost time.

Muslims use the lunar calendar and accept its quirks. Their feasts are "movable" because they shift all the time. That's why the month of Ramadan falls on a different date from one year to the next.

What **year** are we in?

In the year 2000, Jews were in the year 5760 and the Muslims in the year 1420!

Why? Because year 1 of these religions did not start the same year.

The Jewish calendar took the Creation of the world as the starting point. According to the Bible, creation took place in the year 3760 before our era. This date is symbolic, not scientific.

The Christian calendar is accepted throughout the world. It starts with the birth of Jesus Christ, even though a small error did slip in. Historians think that Jesus was born between the years 6 and 3 B.C. (before Christ). In year 1, in other words, Jesus was already between three and six years old! To avoid complicating things, this error was never corrected.

Year 1 of the Muslim calendar begins with a historical event called the *hijra* (the "migration"). It recalls Muhammad's being sent away from Mecca and his arrival in the town of Medina on July 16, 622.

What are the major Jewish feasts?

The feasts that shape the Jewish year are all special moments. God, the creator of the universe, is the inventor of time. God is present in every minute, hour, day, week, month, year and season. Every instant is an opportunity to encounter God, especially the feasts! The Bible calls them "holy invitations," which means they are appointments with God. The major Jewish feasts are Shabbat (Sabbath), Rosh Hashanah, Yom Kippur, Sukkoth, Hanukkah, Purim, Pesach and Shavuot.

The Sabbath

After six days of work, the Sabbath (Shabbat) is celebrated. No one is allowed to work on this day; it is a holy day dedicated to God. *Sabbath* comes from the Hebrew verb meaning "to rest." As it was written in the Bible: "In six days the Lord made heaven and earth, and on the seventh day he rested, and was refreshed" (Exodus 31:19).

According to biblical tradition, God made human beings his partners. By their work, they take part in Creation. But this is not to become a hardship. By resting on the seventh day, God offers human beings a day of "unemployment," a day of rest.

Observe the Sabbath – this is the fourth of the Ten Commandments. The Sabbath is usually described as the day when "you can't do this, you can't do that." Jews who observe the Sabbath do not sow, work, write, start or extinguish fires (or use electricity), use a hammer, and so on. They avoid creating or transforming the state of anything, such as vegetables into soup, logs into ashes, dough into pizza. All week, humans control the Earth. The Sabbath tries to control that creative power that is humanity.

How do Jews celebrate the Sabbath?

The Sabbath begins on Friday evening, one hour before sunset. At that moment, Jews set aside the busyness of the week and stop working. The mother of the home lights two candles, which are signs that a new light illumines the Sabbath. The father goes to the synagogue to "welcome" the Sabbath, which is compared to a bride. Near the middle of the synagogue service, each man turns to the door and sings, "Let's go, my beloved, to meet the bride, and let us welcome the presence of *Shabbat*." Everyone bows to the left and to the right to symbolically greet the "bride-Sabbath." Jewish tradition says that Creation is like a canopy built in six days for a marriage ceremony between the people of God and the "bride-Sabbath."

When the father returns home from the synagogue, he finds a festive table. Before the meal he blesses the wine and two loaves of sweet bread, because God gives twofold on this day. The meal is eaten with joy and songs.

All day Saturday is devoted to prayer, to study of the Torah, and especially to enjoying each other's company. During the Sabbath, all the pressures of the workweek are set aside to focus on hospitality and visiting the sick, for example.

The end of the Sabbath on Saturday evening is marked by a blessing over the wine, aromatic spices and the flame. Weekly activities can be taken up again until the following Sabbath.

Pesach

Pesach is the feast of the Passover, the oldest and most important Jewish feast. It lasts for seven to eight days, starting on the fifteenth day of Nisan (in March–April), and celebrates the escape from Egypt, the founding event of the Jewish people. This people, enslaved by Pharaoh, was led by their leader, Moses, out of Egypt. In the passage from slavery to freedom ("passage" is one meaning for the word *pesach*), this people truly became a nation. *Pesach* also celebrates the birth of Israel.

The key moment is the Passover meal. This meal is called a *Seder*, which means "order," because in the middle of the table the food is arranged in a certain order. It is rich in symbolism. There is *matzah* (unleavened bread), because the people left Egypt so quickly that the bread did not have time to rise; some parsley, a bitter herb, in memory of the bitterness of slavery, and salt water to recall the tears the people shed; a fruit and nut mixture that resembles the mortar the Hebrews used to make bricks; and a roasted lamb shankbone that recalls the lamb the people ate in haste before fleeing.

During this time there is a reading from the *Haggadah* that tells the story of how God freed the people from Egypt. This story is introduced by the youngest family member, who asks the father, "How is this night different from all other nights?" Then the story begins …

Rosh Hashanah

Rosh Hashanah means "head of the year." It is the celebration of the Jewish New Year and takes place on the first or second day of the month of Tishri (in September–October).

Rosh Hashanah celebrates the anniversary of Creation. A text read during the blowing of the *shofar* or ram's horn announces, "Today is the birthday of the world; today God calls to his court all the creatures of the Earth." For Jews, this is an opportunity to take stock of the past year and think about what led them away from God because, at Rosh Hashanah, God examines the hearts of the living. In a very beautiful prayer, Jews speak of God as a shepherd who visits his flock and counts the lambs. As the psalm reminds us, God is "slow to anger and full of love."

Yom Kippur

Yom Kippur is the Day of Atonement. This means God forgives all who turn to him. As you can imagine, this is a very important feast for Jews!

This journey began on the night of the Jewish New Year, because Rosh Hashanah and Yom Kippur are two inseparable feasts. The one indicates the path to take, the other the summit to reach. And between them are ten days of "walking" so people can change their hearts and be reconciled to one another. Only after this happens is God's forgiveness possible.

The day of Yom Kippur is marked by prayer, fasting and asking forgiveness. No work or entertainment should distract the believer from this "holy day."

Sukkoth

This word means a "temporary dwelling." This feast, which takes place between the 15th and 21st day of the month of Tishri (in September–October), recalls that the Israelites, after leaving Egypt, stayed in temporary shelters in the middle of the desert. To celebrate this feast, Jews have to live for seven days in the *sukkah*, a shelter they can set up in their yard or on their balcony. During the service at the synagogue, a bouquet of four types of plants is shaken at the four points of the compass, first upward then downward, to show that God is the king of the entire universe. On the seventh day, people celebrate by singing and dancing.

Hanukkah

This feast, which takes place from the 25th day of the month of Kislev to the third day of the month of Tevet (in November–December), recalls the rededication of the Temple after the victory of the Maccabees over the Greeks. Hanukkah means "to dedicate."

What happened? In the second century B.C., Jerusalem was occupied by Greek soldiers, and Jewish worship was forbidden. The Greek king had even put a statue of Zeus, a Greek god, in the Temple. A Jew named Judas Maccabee was able to liberate Jerusalem. During the eight-day ceremony to purify the Temple, the lamp miraculously stayed lit the whole time, even though there was very little oil left. This is why the Hanukkah lamp is a candlestick with eight branches that is used only for this feast.

Purim

Purim means "lot." This feast recalls Esther's great victory over the Persian king's minister Haman. It took place on the 14th and 15th days of the month of Adar (in February–March). During the reign of Ahasuerus, in the fifth century B.C., Haman planned to kill all the Jews in the empire. He had cast lots (using *purim*, or dice) to decide what day to kill them. The date set was the 13th Adar. But Queen Esther, who was Jewish, begged the king to spare the Jews. Ahasuerus then ordered Haman to be hanged.

To prepare for this celebration, Jews fast the evening before. The next day, at the synagogue, they interrupt the reading from the Book of Esther with noisemakers each time they hear the name of Haman. This popular feast has a carnival atmosphere that brings much joy to children.

Shavuot

Shavuot means "weeks." This feast is celebrated seven weeks after Pesach, that is, 50 days after Passover. In Greek this is translated as "Pentecost," which means "50th."

This feast is mainly about the giving of the Torah (Christians celebrate the giving of the Holy Spirit at Pentecost). Shavuot calls to mind that the Hebrew people, wandering in the desert, received the tablets of the Law, the Torah, on their 50th day of freedom. These are the Ten Commandments. For Jews, the Torah is a true gift from God. It symbolizes their spiritual freedom.

The day is marked by profound joy. Some believers even spend the night studying the Torah, rejoicing at this priceless legacy. Synagogues and homes are decorated with flowers and greenery because the Torah is like a "tree of life."

What are the major Christian feasts?

If you were to ask young Christians what they think the greatest Christian feast is, they would probably say **Christmas**! This is not surprising, because children love Christmas. And this day is special for Christians of all ages, since they celebrate the birth of Jesus in Bethlehem.

But the greatest Christian feast is **Easter**, which celebrates the resurrection of Jesus after his death. If Christ had not appeared alive to his disciples on the third day after being crucified and placed in the tomb, there wouldn't be any Christians! This is why the Church places so much emphasis on "Holy Week," which leads up to this feast – especially Holy Thursday, when they recall the Last Supper, Jesus' last meal with his twelve apostles, and Good Friday, the day he was put to death on a cross.

There are other Christian feasts throughout the year. Shortly after Christmas, **Epiphany** remembers the adoration of the infant Jesus by the Magi

from the East. This is a way of showing that the Son of God came among us to save all of humanity.

Forty days after Easter is **Ascension**, which remembers that Jesus returned to his Father after entrusting his mission to the disciples. Ten days later comes the feast of **Pentecost**. On that day, the 50th after Easter, Jesus' disciples received the Holy Spirit, who gave them the courage to go into the world to proclaim the Good News of Christ.

The Church does not celebrate only Jesus. Catholics also celebrate Mary on August 15, the day of her **Assumption**, her rising to heaven after her death (the Orthodox call this the **Dormition** of the Virgin). **All Saints**, on November 1, is the feast of all those who tried to live holy lives as Jesus asked.

The Orthodox celebrate with great solemnity the feast of the **Transfiguration** (August 6), which recalls the moment when Jesus appeared trans-figured to his disciples, and 40 days later the feast of the **Exaltation of the Holy Cross** (September 14).

Why don't Christians around the world celebrate Christmas on the same day?

Because not all Christians use the same calendar. After the Eastern and Western Churches separated, the West went from the "Julian" calendar, created by Julius Caesar in 45 B.C., to the "Gregorian" calendar, created by Pope Gregory XIII in 1582. But many Eastern countries and Churches kept the Julian calendar, which is out of sync with the new calendar by thirteen days. This difference applies to most of the feasts during the year, except for those connected with Easter. To set the date for Easter, most Christians turn to the Jewish calendar, which follows the cycles of the moon.

What is the difference between Passover and Easter?

When Jesus went up to Jerusalem a few days before being arrested and condemned to death, it was to celebrate the Passover. This great Jewish feast recalls the Hebrew people's exodus from Egypt and their passage from slavery to freedom. With his friends, Jesus took part in the Passover meal. During this meal, which is called the *seder*, Jesus blessed the bread and wine. These blessings are still recited by Jews today. But the blessings would soon take on a new meaning for Christians. That's because Jesus added this: "Take and eat; this is my body.... Take and drink, this is my blood of the covenant, which is poured out for many" (Matthew 26:26-28). (These words are repeated at every Catholic Mass.)

EASTER, A WORD THAT MEANS FREEDOM

The Hebrew word *pesach*, which is translated into English as "Passover," means "passage": for Jews, it is the passage from slavery to freedom; for Christians, it is the passage from death to life. In fact, the two religions are saying the same thing: all are invited to leave slavery and the "prison of suffering" behind and to go beyond death. God wants to break the chains of evil and set us free.

Jesus was then condemned to death and crucified. But three days later, on Easter morning, after
rising from the dead, he appeared first to Mary Mag-
dalene and then to his disciples. This was the resurrection. On Easter, Christians celebrate the resurrection of Jesus – his passage from death to life.

What does the
Star of David stand for?

This six-pointed star is the best-known symbol of Judaism. It is found on the blue and white flag of Israel. Known in Hebrew as the "shield of David," it is believed to have been the royal seal of King Solomon. David and Solomon are the two greatest kings of Israel, which gives you an idea how important that star is for Jews.

This star has several meanings. Here are three of them.

The star has six points representing the six days of Creation. The centre is the seventh day, the day God rested, the Sabbath.

Formed with two intersecting triangles, this star is also a sign of the covenant between God and humankind: the triangle with the point to the bottom is the people. They receive the graces and love that God, the triangle with the point to the top, pours out on them.

This star also represents the messiah that the Jews are waiting for. The Bible says he will come from the house or family of King David.

A TERRIBLE USE OF THE STAR

During the Second World War, the Nazi regime forced Jews to sew a yellow star on their clothing. This was profoundly humiliating. Now that they were identified as Jews for all to see, it made it easier to arrest them for no reason at all and send them to concentration camps. Six million Jews were killed during the war.

Why is the Orthodox cross different from the Catholic cross?

For centuries, the cross has been the symbol of the Christian faith. That was not always the case. In the early Church, the distinctive sign was the fish. The Greek word for fish, *ichthus*, combined the first letters of "Jesus Christ, Son of God, Saviour." Many people did not like the image of the cross because it represented a horrible instrument of torture.

But the cross became widely known, and by the fourth century it was the most recognizable Christian sign. It took different forms, depending on the region and traditions.

In general, a Catholic cross is bare or has the figure of Christ on it (this is called a crucifix). The cross has just one horizontal arm. The Orthodox generally add two more arms: above the large bar (the one on which Jesus' arms are fixed) is a small horizontal arm displaying his name; and below is a small, slightly slanted arm on which his feet rest. Some people like to say that these two arms stand for the two robbers who were crucified at the same time as Christ: one was a good man, the other bad. Most Protestants prefer a simple cross. There is, however, a "Huguenot cross" (from the name of the Protestants in the south of France during the time of the Wars of Religion) on which a dove, the symbol of the Holy Spirit, is attached.

What are the major Muslim feasts?

There are many Muslim feasts.

The Islamic New Year begins on the first day of Muharram, which is the first month of the Islamic year of the lunar or *hijra* calendar. Muhammad left Mecca in 622 to go to the town that is today called Medina. The year 622 marks the date of the **hijra**, which in Arabic means "exile."

The second feast is called **Mawlid** or Mawlid al-Nabi. It celebrates the birth of the prophet Muhammad on the twelfth day of Rabi-al-Awwal, the third month of the year.

The third feast for Muslims is **Ramadan**, the month of fasting. Each day the fast is broken after sunset, and families and friends gather for a meal and some fun together.

The fourth feast, or *eid*, is **Eid al-Fitr**. Also called the "Lesser Feast," it marks the end of Ramadan and includes a special prayer at the mosque between dawn and midday. This feast falls on the first day of Shawwal, the tenth month on the Islamic calendar.

The fifth feast is **Eid al-Adha**, which is also known as the "Greater Feast."

It recalls the willingness of Abraham to sacrifice his son Ishmael before God intervened and gave him a ram to sacrifice instead. Eid al-Adha falls on the tenth day of Dhu al-Hijjah, the last month of the year.

There is also a sixth feast that is celebrated by the Shiite community. This minority group within Islam is found mostly in Iran, but also in Lebanon, Afghanistan, India and Pakistan. The feast is called *Ashura* and it commemorates the martyrdom of Husayne. Husayne was the grandson of the Prophet, whose cousin Ali had married Fatima, the Prophet's daughter. When Ali died, Husayne wanted to lead the community, but others didn't agree. They pursued Husayne for 20 years, finally torturing and killing him. Shiites around the world remember this event during the feast of Ashura. It is a day of mourning.

Why is there a **crescent** on the **flags** of some **Muslim countries**?

The crescent has a link to the lunar calendar that Muslims follow. This distinctive Muslim symbol is different from the Christian symbol, the cross of Jesus, and from the Jewish symbol, the star of David.

Algeria, Pakistan, Tunisia and Turkey are a few of the countries that have the crescent on their flag. The five-pointed star symbolizes the five pillars of Islam. This is not to be confused with the Israeli flag's six-pointed star, which calls to mind the six days of Creation.

Why do **Muslims** wear a **hand-shaped** medal?

Muslims do not wear this medal around their neck; this is an ancient popular tradition among North Africans.

This medal is known as "Fatima's hand." It is simply a good-luck charm, just like the rabbit's foot in other parts of the world. This charm is based on legends, popular myths and superstition, and is not part of Muslim religious beliefs.

Chapter 6

Sacred places

Believers can speak to God wherever they are.
But they also like to gather in certain places so
they can share their faith with others.

Why do they say there is a holy land?

For monotheistic religions, it is not the land itself (soil, stones, sand, dust) that is sacred. (Animistic religions do worship these physical elements.)

What is "holy," or "connected directly to God," are the places where the faithful believe that God has manifested himself and where he remains in a special way.

People venerate or honour places that are directly linked to a revelation of God because they are filled with a very powerful spiritual memory. This is why believers like to make pilgrimages to their "holy land": they can be united even more closely with God and with all the people who have come to this place before them.

A religion may see as "holy" vast spaces, such as countries, where God has appeared to people in some way; cities where major religious figures lived; and places where supernatural phenomena such as apparitions have occurred.

Other "sacred places" include buildings linked to worship, such as temples and shrines, or the places of birth or burial of people who lived holy lives.

Do Christians have a holy land?

According to the Christian faith, God is everywhere. No place is better than another for praying to God. Jesus said that the important thing is not to worship in the Temple of Jerusalem or in any other famous holy place, but to pray "in spirit and in truth" wherever you happen to be.

But Christians have great affection for the land where Jesus lived in the midst of his people. They call it the Holy Land in memory of the centuries of history of the people of Israel who responded to God's call and because Christ himself lived there. He was born in Bethlehem, taught and worked in Galilee, and died and rose again in Jerusalem.

Why is Jerusalem a holy city for Muslims?

For Muslims, Jerusalem is the city of the first monotheistic religions. Until 622, during the first period of Muhammad's preaching, Muslims prayed facing Jerusalem, not Mecca. Also, it was from Jerusalem that Muhammad, in a dream, soared up to heaven on his horse Al-Buraq to meet God and the angels before returning to the earth. This "night of power" (*Laylat al-Qadr,* in Arabic) has been called "better than a thousand months." This is why Muslims venerate Jerusalem. When Mohammad was forced into exile in Medina in 622, Muslims began to pray facing Mecca.

This city is also dear to Muslims because the caliph Omar, the Prophet's second successor, brought Islam to the Near East as far as Jerusalem, where he built the famous Mosque of Omar beside the Al-Aqsa Mosque. Today this spot is called the Mosque Esplanade.

JERUSALEM FOR JEWS AND CHRISTIANS

For Jews, Jerusalem is a holy city because that is where King Solomon built the Temple, the place where God lived among his people.

Christians venerate Jerusalem as the city where Christ was crucified and where it was proclaimed for the first time that God had raised him from the dead.

Do **Christians** have other **holy cities**?

Christians have a strong attachment to cities where the key events of Christianity happened, first during the life of Christ and then during the mission work of the apostles. What Christians experienced in these places is what is venerated, rather than the places themselves. Christians have special respect for the Church of Jerusalem, which is the "Mother" of all the Churches that were formed from her throughout the world, and for the Church of Rome, where the apostles Peter and Paul were martyred for the faith. That is why the bishop of Rome has supreme authority in the Church: he is the pope as well as the successor of Saint Peter, who was the first among the apostles.

Why do many Jews live in Israel?

Jews have lived in countries all over the world for 25 centuries. But they have a special connection with Israel. It is not like any other country.

The history of the Jewish people began with the covenant between God and Abraham. God said to Abraham: "I will give to you, and to your offspring after you, all the land of Canaan, for a perpetual holding" (Genesis 17:8). That's where the expression "Promised Land" comes from.

In this land, the people of Israel had times of prosperity and times of hardship. The most difficult time was when the people were deported to Babylon in 587 B.C. Centuries later, in 70 A.D., the Romans destroyed the Temple of Jerusalem and forced the Jews to leave their country. This is known as the Diaspora. It lasted until the 20th century. During that period, the Jews were persecuted by Christians and by Muslims, almost everywhere in the world. Jews still dreamed of having a land of their own.

In the 20th century, the idea continued to grow. They wanted to return to Palestine, the land of Canaan, the land promised to Abraham. After the terrible persecution of Jews during the Second World War, Palestine was divided between Jews and Arabs in 1948, and the State of Israel was created. But it hasn't been easy. Since then, there hasn't been lasting peace between Israelis and Palestinians in that land.

Why do Jews go and pray in front of a wall in Jerusalem?

The Wall (*kotel* in Hebrew), also called the Western Wall (*HaKotel HaMa'aravi*), is about 100 metres long. It is the holiest place in Jerusalem, even though it wasn't part of the ancient Temple, as many people think. It is all that remains of the western foundation of the walkway of the Temple, the place where God had established his dwelling and that was the heart of Israel's life. It was destroyed by the Romans in 70 A.D.

Jews would pray at the wall, expressing their sadness about the destruction of the Temple. (That is why it used to be called the Wailing Wall.) They would repeat the words of Isaiah: "Our holy and beautiful house, where our ancestors praised you, has been burned by fire, and all our pleasant places have become ruins" (64:11).

This majestic wall is no longer a source of wailing. It is a place where God is present. Jews come and pray there today as if they are in an open-air synagogue.

What is a **pilgrimage**?

For believers, a pilgrimage is a journey to a holy place: a village, a sacred river, a miraculous well, a gravesite, a spot in the desert or a mountaintop.

It all begins with the departure: you have to leave, to set out on the road, to take up your pilgrim's staff. But why do believers set out? There are many reasons: to give thanks, ask for forgiveness, make a vow, heal, find answers, and more.

Pilgrims often set out searching for God, even if they don't believe in God. They don't have all the answers; they are seekers. A pilgrimage is a faith journey. You could say that the path they travel is very much like life: it has moments of both joy and hardship.

All pilgrims say that when they arrive at the end of their journey, which can be quite long, they are no longer the same. Whether they go to Mecca, Jerusalem or Lourdes, something has changed in them. This change is often hard to explain, because it is so personal. Did the pilgrims find God? Maybe. But they have found themselves, and this is a great source of peace and joy.

THE WAY OF SAINT JAMES

In the last 25 years or so, the pilgrimage to the shrine of Saint James (in Spanish, *Santiago*) in Compostela, Spain, has again become one of the three main Christian pilgrimages, along with the ones to Rome and Jerusalem. It is very popular among young people. There is a huge church in Compostela where, tradition says, the body of Saint James, the first apostle to lay down his life for Jesus, is buried.

Beginning in the year 1000, roads and bridges were built, along with guesthouses to welcome the poor, comfort the sick, and shelter pilgrims from bandits. There are five routes across Europe leading to Compostela.

Why do Muslims go on a pilgrimage to Mecca?

Pilgrimage (*hajj* in Arabic) is the fifth and final pillar of the faith (see page 60), but only Muslims who are in good health and have enough money are expected to make this pilgrimage. Mecca is not the only place of pilgrimage for Muslims. There is also Medina, the town where Muhammad died and is buried.

Muslims distinguish between minor and major pilgrimages. The minor pilgrimage is only to Mecca. The major pilgrimage includes Mecca, Medina and Mount Arafat, the hill above Mecca where Muhammad received his first sermon from the archangel Gabriel.

Those who make this pilgrimage have the right to add the title *hajji* to their name. This means they are recognized by the community as people whose words and actions are worthy of imitation. In a sense, these are holy men and holy women.

Do people have to make pilgrimages?

Jews used to be required to go the Temple of Jerusalem three times a year for pilgrimage celebrations: Pesach, Shavuot and Sukkoth. But the Temple no longer exists. To make a pilgrimage is now a personal choice, not a requirement. For Christians, pilgrimages are popular. Pilgrims are travellers, strangers, like Jesus was in his country. Protestant Christians are not as interested in pilgrimages, because they distrust the way that some people make pilgrimages to "bargain" with God so that something good will happen in their lives. For Muslims, the pilgrimage to Mecca is one of the Five Pillars of Islam. They fulfill this religious duty at least once in their lifetime if they can afford it and their health is good.

Chapter 7

CURRENT ISSUES

Some believers do terrible things in the name of
God. Still, faithful Jews, Christians and Muslims
want all people to be happy …

Why do **Muslim women** have fewer rights than **Muslim men**?

Islam began in a society made up of a number of tribes that had certain rules. For example, women were not allowed to inherit property, so it could be kept within the tribe. Islam made things better for women: the Prophet decreed that women could inherit half of the man's share. This decree was added to the Qur'an in writing 20 years after Muhammad's death. This meant it was like a word from God dictated to the Prophet by the archangel Gabriel, and couldn't be changed.

In these same tribes, women's only purpose was to bear children. That is why a man had the right to as many wives as he wished, and could abandon them whenever he wanted. Islam outlined laws for marriage along with the rights and duties of the woman. The wife of the Prophet, to whom he promised to be faithful until her death in 619 A.D., was a prominent businesswoman.

The woman's role is always to have children, since it says in the Qur'an, "Your women are your fields. Go, then, into your fields as you will." When it comes to rights, the Qur'an says that "wives have rights corresponding to those which the husbands have, according to what is recognized to be fair, but men have a rank above them" (*sura* 2:228). For example, a woman's testimony as a witness is worth half of a man's (*sura* 2:282). A man has the right to repudiate his spouse; a woman does not have this right (*sura* 2:227). And a woman may not marry a non-Muslim, but a man may do so as long as his wife is a practising Christian or Jew. When it comes to prayer, men and women are equal.

Why are there no **women priests**?

When you read the Gospels, it is clear that the twelve apostles, chosen by Jesus to proclaim the Good News to the world, were men. For a very long time, all Christians agreed that priests and bishops, as Church leaders, also had to be men. But, beginning in the nineteenth century, Protestants began to appoint women as pastors. More recently, Anglicans began to ordain women as priests and even bishops. For them, Jesus' choice of men can be explained by the culture of his time, when women were not seen as equal to men. For these Churches, because women's rights and dignity are recognized today, there is no reason they should not be ordained.

Catholics and Orthodox do not see things this way. For them, Christ truly wanted the apostles, and therefore the priests and bishops who came after them, to be men, because they were somehow identified with Jesus through their ordination. This doesn't mean that women are second-class Christians! They are becoming more and more involved in the Christian community: for example, by taking on various leadership roles and teaching adults and children about the faith. Even if women cannot be priests, they offer many gifts and talents that the Church needs.

What is fanaticism?

Some believers think that their religion offers the only way of looking at the world. This attitude is called fundamentalism or religious fanaticism. It gives exaggerated importance to the laws of that religion, which they want to impose, sometimes by force, on an entire society.

Over the past number of years, religious fanaticism has grown. In some countries, extremists are fighting in the name of Islam or Judaism. In Northern Ireland, Catholics and Protestants have been clashing for decades. Religion is used to justify the violence.

The most dramatic example of this occurred on September 11, 2001, in New York. Fanatics admitted that they carried out these attacks against a Western Christian civilization in the name of Allah. But behind their actions was a political goal: to attack American economic power.

Fifteen years earlier, in 1986, Pope John Paul II invited the leaders of many religions to meet in Assisi to condemn any kind of attack and to affirm that violence cannot be committed and justified in the name of God.

Should we be afraid of **fundamentalists**?

Religious fanatics are often even more dangerous than some extremist political movements, because these fanatics think God is ordering them to act this way. Of course, this same danger does not exist when these believers apply their religious laws only to themselves, or when they think that everyone should believe and act as they do but do not use violence to impose their faith on other people.

But even when they don't go to these extremes, religious fundamentalists can frighten people. They think religion works by exclusion: according to them, either you are right or you are wrong. But things are not that black and white: all religions emphasize a part of truth that the others overlook or underestimate. They also think their faith calls them to act in society in certain ways, which sometimes means they disobey the law and threaten public safety. Some people who support the Islamic headscarf, for example, are convinced that women should wear it because God ordered this and therefore no human law can oppose it. But every society must be able to run in peace and harmony. On the one hand, the state must recognize the freedom of all citizens to belong to the religion of their choice; on the other hand, believers must agree not to impose their own beliefs and practices on everyone else.

What is a **holy war**?

"Holy war" is often mentioned in connection with Islam, but what is said is not always correct.

To practise Islam is to surrender oneself to God. The Prophet Muhammad clearly said that he was the last of the prophets, that he had come to perfect religion, and that he would like Islam to be the religion of all believers. He was speaking both to believers who had come before him and to those who would live after him. For Muhammad, the future of humanity was to put itself in God's hands. Of course, in surrendering to God, the world's borders would disappear and the world would once again be a large community without borders – the *umma*. Creating this community is the ultimate goal of Islam.

The idea of a holy war came later. The word *jihad*, which is translated as "holy war," never meant "war." The Arabic word for war is *harb*. *Jihad* comes from the root word *jhd*, which means "effort." The great *jihad* is the effort a person makes to be a good Muslim and to ensure that his family are good Muslims, too. It is also the effort he makes so that those who have not yet surrendered to God will do so, because it is for their own good. It is in this sense that the word *jihad* has come to mean holy war, and is used today to explain all Muslim conflicts.

Do **believers** have the **right to kill**?

Every religion has this divine commandment: "You shall not kill." Why? Because life comes from God, and it must return to God. Life is sacred – it's the greatest good there is. No one has the right to dispose of life however they want. All ways of killing are forbidden: murder, suicide, revenge killings, capital punishment, letting people die by not feeding or caring for them, abortion and euthanasia.

In today's world, there are signs that point to a "culture of death." We do not always respect and value life as we should. Believers must be among the first to refuse all these ways of killing.

There is one case where this issue is debated a lot: war. In a war, people are killed. So do religions forbid every kind of war? No. They say that "just wars" are possible, but only under certain conditions: if the proper authorities say it is for a good reason; if all peaceful solutions have been tried and have failed; if it does not cause more harm than good; and if everything possible is done to protect innocent civilians.

Can people change their religion?

Of course! Everyone can practise the religion of their choice, either because it is the religion they were born into or because they have decided that path is the best for their spiritual growth.

The religions themselves should make this clear, but none of them wants to see their members leave to join other religious groups. It can be complicated to change religions. For example, to be a Jew is not first a personal choice, but the result of being born into a particular people. One cannot choose to stop being a Jew, only to stop participating in the faith and rituals of the Jewish people. But someone who is not a Jew can convert to Judaism.

Each religion has developed a number of rules to help converts fit in. To become a Jew, a person must commit to observing the Torah and undergoing certain rituals: immersion in a ritual bath, circumcision (for men), and so on. To become a Christian, a person must go through a period of initiation (called the catechumenate) before receiving the first sacraments: baptism, confirmation and eucharist. To become a Muslim, a person needs to purify themselves by washing and publicly make the profession of faith that opens the Qur'an.

What do Jews say about Christians and Muslims?

Christians and Muslims can be considered the "younger siblings" of the Jews because it is said that Judaism is "the mother" of these religions that also promote belief in one God. This belief is "our common trunk," say the Jews, and Christianity and Islam are its branches.

The Bible says that God gave the Jewish people this vocation of making him known throughout the Earth, to be "a torch-bearer nation" that can testify to God, the Most High.

In the same way, Christians and Muslims are seen as partners, because they actively contribute in spreading knowledge of God. This is how humanity moves toward goodness, peace and fraternity. Of course, the paths are different, but these religions are of enormous value. One might say they "advertise" humanity by demonstrating and fostering what is beautiful in human beings.

Jews and Christians speak the same language – the language of the Bible. The same stories and people nourish their faith. Christians need Jews in order to understand better who they really are, and to know Jesus better, because he was a Jew who was shaped by the history of Israel. Jews cannot ignore Christianity, which was grafted onto them and draws from the same roots.

Some Jews still distrust Christians because of the serious anti-Jewish (or anti-Semitic) attitudes Christians held in the past. Today, many relationships are developing between Jews and Christians. They call for dialogue that is full of respect and hope.

Jews and Muslims have lived together in the Middle East and North Africa for a long time. Many similarities exist in their religious practices in the life of believers, dietary laws, religious purity laws and circumcision. But Jews disagree with the way Muslims put religious law ahead of civil law in the country where they live, since this always leads to clashes with the authorities. The existence of the state of Israel causes conflict between Jews and Muslims. In that country, Israelis and Palestinians (who are mostly Muslim) have been clashing for many years and still have not been able to find a solution that leads to long-term peace and understanding.

What do Christians say about Jews and Muslims?

They believe in the same God and recognize each other as "children of Abraham," but Christians do not look at Jews and Muslims in exactly the same way.

Christianity was indeed born from Judaism. Jesus himself was Jewish, as were his apostles and first disciples, and the message of the Gospel is rooted in Jewish Law, the Torah, which God revealed to Moses. That is why the Christian Bible includes both the Old Testament (the first covenant made by God with the people of Israel) and the New Testament.

But, at the same time, Christianity sees itself as fulfilling Judaism. Jesus said that he did not come to abolish the Law, but to fulfill it. For the Church, he is the Christ, the Messiah that the Jewish people are waiting for. He is the very Word of God who became human.

This is why Christians see Jews as their older siblings, but as we can see from history, Christians did not always respect these siblings. For a long time, many Christians blamed the Jewish people for the death of Jesus, and they used this as a reason to persecute the Jews. Today, fortunately, the Church strongly condemns this anti-Semitism.

The prophet Muhammad founded a religion that was said to be inspired by God to fulfill both Judaism and Christianity. This is why the Qur'an often speaks of Moses, Mary and Jesus, whom Muslims venerate as a prophet. For the Church, however, it is Christ who personifies this fulfillment. Also, for Christians it is a problem that Islam blends religion and politics without always separating personal beliefs from how their society is governed. And Christians find it a serious problem that they are not always allowed to worship freely and publicly in certain countries that have a strong Muslim tradition. Still, the Church respects Islam and the spiritual growth it makes possible for so many people around the world.

What do Muslims say about Jews and Christians?

Islam calls the members of the other monotheistic religions "the people of the Book" (*ahl al-kitab*, in Arabic). After his exile from Mecca, the Prophet Muhammad, on arriving in Medina, hoped to find support from the city's three Jewish tribes. Weren't they monotheists? Didn't they claim to be descendants of Abraham, too?

This same attitude of openness toward Christians was seen from the very beginning of his preaching. In 631, a year before his death, the Prophet himself signed an agreement with the large Christian community at the oasis of Najran. In return, he asked them to pay a special tax to be under the protection of the *umma*, the community of Muslim believers.

The Qur'an clearly states that there will be no "compulsion in religion" – people can follow their individual conscience. But as the years passed, things got worse for the people of the Book: warnings and threats toward Jews and Christians increased. Jews were accused of turning away from the Scriptures: "Those who were charged with bearing the Torah but did not do so are like an ass carrying a load of books" (*sura* 62, verse 5).

The charge against Christians was even stronger – they were seen as blasphemers: "In blasphemy indeed are those who say, 'God is Christ, the son of Mary'" (*sura* 5, verse 17).

The same *sura* adds: "They are deniers of the truth who say, 'God is one of three.' There is only

one God" (verse 73). Still, Islam made Jews and Christians *dhimmis*, protected citizens of the Muslim community.

After the death of the Prophet in 632, his second successor, the caliph Omar, signed the agreement that bears his name with Christians in Syria and Palestine. This document required these other believers to "live in a state of humiliation," which goes against the agreement made at Najran.

Can you be involved in politics without talking about your religion?

In the Gospel, Jesus said, "Give to the emperor the things that are the emperor's, and to God the things that are God's" (Mark 12:17). For Christians, the message is clear: they can be involved in political life without mentioning their faith. A Christian's relationship with God is personal.

But this attitude is not accepted by all believers, including Christians themselves. Some believers do not hesitate to talk about their faith to make themselves look good or to impose their religious point of view on society.

This is especially noticeable in Muslim countries today. For the past few years, Muslims have been turning more and more to religion to give themselves new signposts in daily life. Their countries, which had believed in politics without involving religion, have gone through some difficult times. Some Muslims think that solutions to their country's problems can only come from Islam. This can be seen in Iran, Afghanistan and Pakistan. This is how religious intolerance is born (see page 28).

In Judaism, the ancient traditions always blended politics and religion. The creation of the state of Israel in 1948 has made the situation more complex. Israel was created to welcome persecuted Jews from around the world. This country has laws that come directly from the Jewish religious tradition.

This leads to some important questions: Could anyone who is not a Muslim be the leader of a Muslim state? Could a non-Jew lead the State of

Israel? Could anyone take on the highest political office of a largely Christian country without being a Christian?

It would be difficult, if not impossible! The only notable exception is Western countries, where a politician is free to believe or not to believe: this is not an obstacle to a political career.

We can only hope that in the 21st century, Judaism, Christianity and Islam will find ways to work and live together that will spread God's message of love and mercy for all people.

Appendixes

GLOSSARY AND INDEX

A

Abraham: father of all believers, 19, 20, 34, 40, 63, 140, 158
Ali (born between 600 and 611): cousin and son-in-law of the prophet Muhammad, 54, 131
All Saints: Christian feast of all the saints (November 1), 123
Allah: "God" in Arabic, 18, 55
Altar, 100, 101
Anglican: 30, 149
Ascension: "risen" in Latin; Christian feast celebrating the ascent of Jesus to his Father 40 days after his **Resurrection**, 123
Ash Wednesday: first day of Lent, 75
Assumption (of the Virgin): "taken up to heaven" in Latin; Christian feast remembering that Mary, the Mother of God, was taken body and soul up to heaven, 123

B

Babylon: Mesopotamian city, now in the south of Iraq, 20, 98, 140
Baptism, Baptize: "to immerse" in Greek, 70, 74
Bar mitzvah: "son of the commandment" in Hebrew; Jewish feast that marks the religious maturity of boys, 65
Bat mitzvah: "daughter of the commandment" in Hebrew, 65
Bible: "the books" in Greek; collection of texts revealed to the people of Israel, 35, 38, 41, 44, 55

C

Calendar, 14, 115, 125
Caliph: "successor" in Arabic; the ruler whose task is to ensure that the prescriptions of the Qur'an reign supreme on Earth, 24, 55, 84, 138, 161
Calvin, John (1509–1564): French Protestant Reformer, 32, 76
Canaan: ancient name of the Promised Land, which became the land of Israel, 20, 140
Catholic, Catholicism: "universal Church" in Greek, 30, 31, 71, 72, 73, 85, 129, 149
Charismatic: "favour" in Latin; movement to renew Christian charisms, 76
Christ: "the messiah, the One sent" in Greek; for Christians, Jesus is the One sent by God, 21, 42, 44, 45, 47, 48, 158
Christian: name given to Christ's disciples, 21
Christmas: Christian feast celebrating the birth of Jesus, the Christ, 122, 125
Church: "assembly" in Greek, 43, 70, 71, 89, 100
Church (building): 100
Circumcision: 64, 63, 155
Covenant: agreement that God made with the prophets and his people; also the name given in the Bible to the Old Testament and the New Testament, 41, 44

Creator God, 14, 37, 82, 94, 99
Creed: from the Latin credo, "I believe"; the Christian proclamation of faith, 42
Cremation, 88, 89, 91
Crescent: Muslim symbol, 132
Cross, Christian symbol, 129
Crucifixion: Roman method of torture that consisted of nailing a person to a post in the form of a cross, 44

D

David: king of Israel around the year 1000 B.C., 128
Deiwo: "God" in Sanskrit, 14
Divorce, 84, 96, 87
Dormition (of the Virgin): Orthodox feast that corresponds to the Assumption of Mary, 123

E

Easter, 46, 75, 122, 126, 127
Eid al-Adha: the "Greater Feast" for Muslims, 131
Eid al-Fitr: the "Lesser Feast" for Muslims, 130
Epiphany: "manifestation" in Greek; feast that commemorates the adoration of the infant Jesus by the Magi, 123
Eucharist: "thanksgiving" in Greek; another name Catholics use for the Mass, 48, 74, 103

F

Fanaticism, 150
Fasting, 58, 130
Fatima's hand, 133
Feasts (religious celebrations), 116, 122, 123, 130, 131
Fundamentalist, 151
Funerals, 88, 89, 91

G

Gabriel, archangel: "man of God" in Hebrew, 24, 53, 144, 148
Gospel: "good news" in Greek; the New Testament accounts about events in the life of Jesus, 44, 102

H

Haggadah: "reading" in Hebrew; the collection of texts that belong to the rabbinic tradition, 119
Hail Mary: Christian prayer, 96
Hajj: "pilgrimage" in Arabic, 144
Halal: "pure meat" in Arabic, 66
Hanukkah: "dedication" in Hebrew; Jewish feast, 120
Headscarf (Islamic), 83, 151
Heaven, 52, 59
Hebrew, 20
Hijab: "veil" in Arabic, 111
Hijra: "exile, migration" in Arabic; corresponds with the expulsion of the prophet Muhammad from Mecca, 115, 130
Holy Ark (also called the Ark of the Covenant): a strongbox that holds the Ten Commandments, 98
Holy Land, 136, 137
Holy Spirit, 43, 49, 50, 72, 108
Holy War, 152
Holy Week: the week preceding Easter, 124

I

Icon: "image" in Greek; for the Orthodox, the icon is a representation of Christ, the Virgin Mary or the saints, 85, 100, 105
Imam: "in front" in Arabic, 80, 106
Isaac: son of Abraham, 19
Isaiah: prophet in the eighth century B.C., 141
Ishmael: son of Abraham, 19
Islam: "peace, health" in Arabic, 23, 81, 159
Islamist, 24, 25
Israel (state of), 20, 28, 62, 63, 140, 157
Israelite, 20

J

Jerusalem, 50, 98, 101, 138, 139, 143
Jesus: the Son of God, 16, 21, 29, 36, 41, 42, 44, 45, 46, 47, 48, 50, 137, 158
Jew, 20
Jewish New Year (see Rosh Hashanah)
Jihad: "effort toward a set goal" in Arabic, 152
John the Baptist: prophet at the time of Jesus, 28
Judaism, 34

K

Kaddish: Jewish prayer, 95
Kadosh: "holy" in Hebrew, 68
Keffiyeh, 99
Ketubah: "marriage contract" in Hebrew, 84
Kingdom of God, 48
Kippah: "dome" in Hebrew; skullcap worn by Jews, 99
Kosher: "suitable" in Hebrew; a term used in various aspects of life, especially for food, 66

L

Last Supper: the final meal that Jesus had with his disciples, 122
Law, or tablets of the Law (see Torah)
Lent: for Christians, the period of 40 days (from Ash Wednesday to Holy Thursday, not counting Sundays) that precedes the feast of Easter, 75, 78
Lourdes: pilgrimage site for Christians that is in the south of France, 143
Luther, Martin (1483–1546): German reformer whose work paved the way for Protestantism to develop, 31, 76
Lutherans, 76

M

Magnificat: "magnify" in Latin; prayer of praise offered by the Virgin Mary, 96
Marriage, 72, 84, 85, 87
Mary (Virgin), mother of Jesus, 43, 49, 50, 103, 108
Mass, 103, 104
Mawlid (or Mawlid an-Nabi): celebration of the birth of the prophet Muhammad, 130
Mecca: city located in Saudi Arabia; it was around Mecca where the prophet Muhammad had his first revelations, 54, 55, 56, 91, 98, 106, 115, 143, 144, 160

Q

Qadi: "marriage contract" in Arabic, 87
Qur'an: "recitation" in Arabic, 24, 52, 54, 56, 58, 80, 87, 91, 97, 106, 107, 110, 148, 155, 159

R

Rabbi, 63, 64, 68, 84, 88
Ramadan: ninth month of the Muslim calendar, 56, 58, 114, 130
Resurrected, Resurrection: "risen" in Greek; for Christians, this is Christ's victory of life over death, 46, 70, 90, 103, 127
Rome, 139
Rosary: beads used in Christian prayer, 96
Rosh Hashanah: Jewish New Year, 119

S

Sabbath (Shabbat), "to rest" in Hebrew; for the Jews, a day of rest consecrated to God, 65, 116, 117
Sacrament, 48, 72, 86
Sacred tetragram: "four letters" in Greek; the four letters (YHWH) in Hebrew that correspond to the name of God, 40
Saint, 68, 73, 81
Seder: "order" in Hebrew, 118, 126
Shabbat (see Sabbath)
Shavuot: "weeks" in Hebrew; Jewish feast, 11, 143
Shema Israel: "Hear, O Israel" in Hebrew; a Jewish prayer, 95
Shofar: musical instrument made from an animal's horn, 119
Sign of the Cross, 102
Sinai: mountain and desert in northeast Egypt, 34, 39
Solomon: king of Israel; son of King David, 128
Star (five-pointed): Muslim symbol, 132
Star of David: Jewish symbol, 128, 134
Sukkoth: "temporary dwelling" in Hebrew; Jewish feast, 120, 143
Sunday: "day of the Lord" in Latin, 103
Synagogue: "house of assembly" in Hebrew, 63, 64, 69, 88, 98, 117, 121

T

Tabernacle, 101
Tallit: Jewish prayer shawl, 99
Temple of Jerusalem, 98, 101, 137, 140, 141, 143, 145
Ten Commandments (or "Ten Words"), the prescriptions that God gave to Moses on Mount Sinai, 34, 38, 39, 121
Testament (Old and New), the two major parts of the Christian Bible, 41, 44, 48, 90, 96, 158
Torah: "the Law" in Hebrew, 34, 36, 38, 39, 41, 52, 62, 64, 68, 98, 117, 121, 154, 158
Transfiguration: Christian feast celebrated on August 6, 123
Trinity: for Christians, the one God in three persons – Father, Son and Holy Spirit, 16, 50, 51, 52, 102
Tzitzit: fringes on the tallit, 99

U

Umma: "community" in Arabic, 82, 152, 160

W

Western Wall, 141
Women, 69, 148, 149
Word of God, 36, 51, 100

Y

Yahweh: God's name in the Bible, 18
YHWH (see also sacred tetragram), 40
Yom Kippur: "Day of Atonement" in Hebrew; Jewish feast, 119

Major historical events

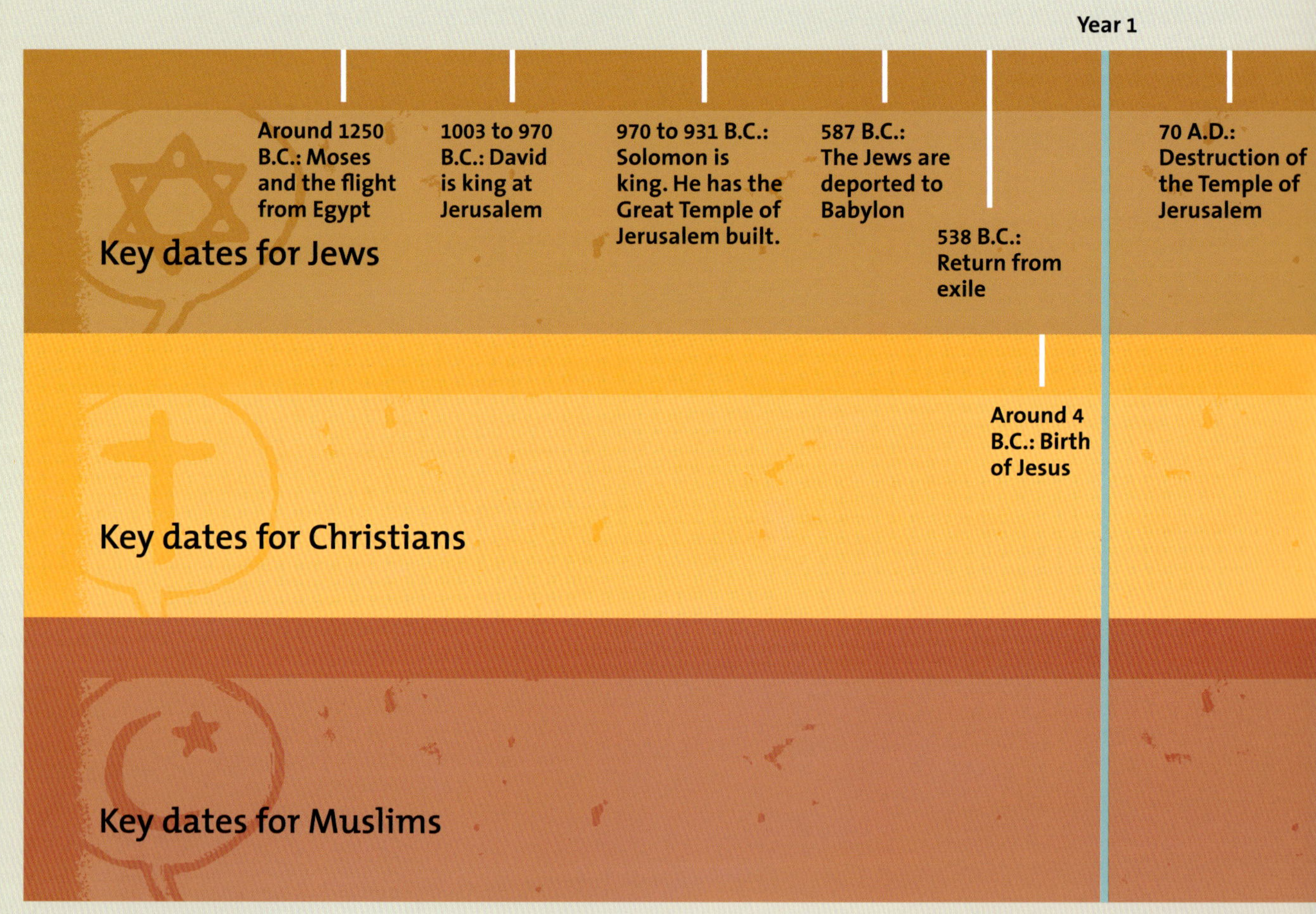

1942: The Nazis, led by Adolf Hitler, decide to exterminate the Jews. In January, the "final solution to the Jewish problem" is planned.

1948: Creation of the state of Israel

313: Edict of Milan: Christians are no longer persecuted

1054: The Great Schism: Eastern Christians and Western Christians separate

1095 to 1270: The Crusades

1517: Martin Luther initiates a great reform movement. It is the birth of Protestantism.

1962 to 1965: Vatican Council II

1978: John Paul II is elected pope

August 20, 570: Birth of Muhammad

622: The Hijra: Muhammad leaves Mecca to take refuge in Medina.

680: The martyrdom of Husayne marks the birth of Shiism

1490: Shiism is declared the state religion in Iran

MAJOR MOVABLE FEASTS

On the Jewish, Christian and Muslim calendars, the major feasts fall on different dates each year.

To help you find them, here are the dates of these feasts from 2013 to 2024. You can enter these dates on the big calendar on pages 184 to 187. During the year, you can keep up with the most important religious feasts of your Jewish, Christian and Muslim friends.

Year	Rosh Hashanah	Yom Kippur	Sukkoth	Hanukkah
5774 (2013–2014)	September 5	September 14	September 19	November 27
5775 (2014–2015)	September 25	October 4	October 9	December 17
5776 (2015–2016)	September 14	September 23	September 27	December 6
5777 (2016–2017)	October 3	October 12	October 16	December 24
5778 (2017–2018)	September 21	September 30	October 4	December 12
5779 (2018–2019)	September 10	September 19	September 23	December 2
5780 (2019–2020)	September 30	October 9	October 13	December 22
5781 (2020–2021)	September 19	September 28	October 2	December 10
5782 (2021–2022)	September 7	September 16	September 20	November 28
5783 (2022–2023)	September 26	October 5	October 9	December 18
5784 (2023–2024)	September 16	September 25	September 28	December 7

Purim	Pesach	Shavuot
March 16	April 13	June 2
March 5	April 3	May 23
March 24	April 20	June 9
March 12	April 19	May 29
March 1	March 30	May 19
March 21	April 19	June 8
March 10	April 7	May 27
February 26	March 26	May 15
March 17	April 15	June 4
March 7	April 14	May 24
March 24	April 23	June 12

Major movable Jewish feasts (2013–2024)

The Jewish calendar is a lunar calendar. Each month lasts for 29 or 30 days. To come up with a year of 365 days, Jews would insert a thirteenth month periodically. This is why the feasts are movable. Year 1, according to tradition, corresponds to the creation of the world.

Year	Ash Wednesday	Catholic and Protestant Easter	Orthodox Easter	Ascension
2013	February 13	March 31	May 5	May 9
2014	March 5	April 20	April 20	May 29
2015	February 18	April 5	April 12	May 14
2016	February 10	March 27	May 1	May 5
2017	March 1	April 16	April 16	May 25
2018	February 14	April 1	April 8	May 10
2019	March 6	April 21	April 28	May 30
2020	February 26	April 12	April 19	May 31
2021	February 17	April 4	May 2	May 13
2022	March 2	April 17	April 24	May 26
2023	February 22	April 9	April 16	May 18

Year	First of Muharram (New Year's Day)	Start of Ramadan	Eid al-Fitr (end of Ramadan)
1435	November 4 2013	June 28 2014	July 28 2014
1436	October 25 2014	June 18 2015	July 17 2015
1437	October 14 2015	June 6 2016	July 6 2016
1438	October 2 2016	May 27 2017	June 25 2017
1439	September 21 2017	May 16 2018	June 15 2018
1440	September 11 2018	May 6 2019	June 4 2019
1441	August 31 2019	April 24 2020	May 24 2020
1442	August 20 2020	April 13 2021	May 13 2021
1443	August 9 2021	April 2 2022	May 2 2022
1444	July 30 2022	March 23 2023	April 21 2023
1445	July 19 2023	March 11 2024	April 10 2024
1446	July 7 2024		

Pentecost	Advent
May 19	December 1
June 8	November 30
May 24	November 29
May 15	November 27
June 4	December 3
May 20	December 2
June 9	December 1
May 31	November 29
May 23	November 28
June 5	November 27
May 28	December 3

Major movable Christian feasts (2013–2024)

Certain Christian feasts are set, such as Christmas (December 25) and Assumption (August 15). The date for Easter is calculated from the movements of the moon and changes from one year to the next. All feasts connected with Easter, such as Ash Wednesday and Pentecost, are movable. Year 1 corresponds to the birth of Jesus.

Eid al-Adha
October 4 2014
September 23 2015
September 11 2016
September 1 2017
August 21 2018
August 11 2019
July 31 2020
July 20 2021
July 9 2022
June 28 2023
June 16 2024

Major movable Muslim feasts (2013–2024)

The Muslim year consists of 12 lunar months of 29 or 30 days each. That makes a total of 354 days, which is 11 days less than a solar year. This means that Muslim feasts move forward by 10 days every year. Year 1 corresponds to the Hijra, the expulsion of Muhammad from Mecca to Medina, in 622.

MY CALENDAR OF RELIGIOUS FEASTS

January		February		March	
1		1		1	
2		2		2	
3		3		3	
4		4		4	
5		5		5	
6		6		6	
7		7		7	
8		8		8	
9		9		9	
10		10		10	
11		11		11	
12		12		12	
13		13		13	
14		14		14	
15		15		15	
16		16		16	
17		17		17	
18		18		18	
19		19		19	
20		20		20	
21		21		21	
22		22		22	
23		23		23	
24		24		24	
25		25		25	
26		26		26	
27		27		27	
28		28		28	
29		29		29	
30				30	
31				31	

April	May	June
1	1	1
2	2	2
3	3	3
4	4	4
5	5	5
6	6	6
7	7	7
8	8	8
9	9	9
10	10	10
11	11	11
12	12	12
13	13	13
14	14	14
15	15	15
16	16	16
17	17	17
18	18	18
19	19	19
20	20	20
21	21	21
22	22	22
23	23	23
24	24	24
25	25	25
26	26	26
27	27	27
28	28	28
29	29	29
30	30	30
	31	

My calendar of religious feasts

July		August		September	
1		1		1	
2		2		2	
3		3		3	
4		4		4	
5		5		5	
6		6		6	
7		7		7	
8		8		8	
9		9		9	
10		10		10	
11		11		11	
12		12		12	
13		13		13	
14		14		14	
15		15		15	
16		16		16	
17		17		17	
18		18		18	
19		19		19	
20		20		20	
21		21		21	
22		22		22	
23		23		23	
24		24		24	
25		25		25	
26		26		26	
27		27		27	
28		28		28	
29		29		29	
30		30		30	
31		31			

October	November	December
1	1	1
2	2	2
3	3	3
4	4	4
5	5	5
6	6	6
7	7	7
8	8	8
9	9	9
10	10	10
11	11	11
12	12	12
13	13	13
14	14	14
15	15	15
16	16	16
17	17	17
18	18	18
19	19	19
20	20	20
21	21	21
22	22	22
23	23	23
24	24	24
25	25	25
26	26	26
27	27	27
28	28	28
29	29	29
30	30	30
31		31

The authors

Katia Mrowiec is a journalist from Poland who has written for a number of religious magazines. She is a member of the Fraternity of Saint Mark, whose goal is to memorize the Word of God according to the Jewish tradition. With the help of Alexis Blum, the Chief Rabbi of the Neuilly-sur-Seine synagogue in Paris, she wrote the answers to the questions about Judaism.

Michel Kubler was born in Alsace. He is an Assumptionist priest, a theologian and the editor-in-chief of the Catholic daily newspaper *La Croix*. For many years he has been interested in the big religious questions of the world. He is especially interested in dialogue that takes place among different Christian traditions and in relations among the world religions. He wrote the answers to the questions about Christianity.

Antoine Sfeir was born in Lebanon. He is a journalist and the editor of the French magazine *Les Cahiers de l'Orient* (Notebooks from the East). He is a specialist in Islam and is often interviewed on televisiown and radio. He is the author of *Atlas des religions* (Atlas of Religions) and *Dictionnaire mondial de l'islamisme* (World Dictionary of Islamism). He wrote the responses to the questions about Islam.